To Ken Swallow, 1931–92, college librarian
Chairman of CoFHE, 1979–82

COLLEGES, LIBRARIES AND ACCESS TO LEARNING

COLLEGES, LIBRARIES AND ACCESS TO LEARNING

Marie Adams and Rennie McElroy, editors

Library Association Publishing
London

Published by
Library Association Publishing Ltd
7 Ridgmount Street
London WC1E 7AE

First published 1994

British Library Cataloguing in Publication Data
A catalogue record for this book is available from the British Library

ISBN 1-85604-072-0

Typeset from editors' disk in 11/12pt Garamond by Library Association Publishing Ltd
Printed and made in Great Britain by Bookcraft (Bath) Ltd

Contents

Contributors   viii
List of abbreviations   ix
Preface   xi

1   The student and the learning process   1
    John Cowan

2   The institutional context; further education   21
    Michael Rowarth

3   The institutional context; higher education   34
    John Stoddart and Simon Hughes

4   Organizing resources for learning   47
    Allen Armsby

5   The role of the librarian in student learning and
    assessment   68
    Paula Kingston

6   The support team approach   84
    Marie Adams

7   The college librarian   98
    Ken Watson and Tim Lomas

8   Quality in college libraries   113
    Rennie McElroy

9   College librarianship and the professional network   129
    Margaret Oldroyd and Robert Oldroyd

10 Looking to the future   140
    Tom Wilson

Contributors

Marie Adams BA MA ALA
Learning Resources Co-ordinator, Barnet College

Allen Armsby BA ALA
Director of Learning Resources, Newcastle College

Dr John Cowan MBE DEng FIStructE FEIS
Scottish Director, The Open University in Scotland

Simon Hughes BA
formerly Administrative Assistant, Sheffield Hallam University
now Barnsley and Doncaster Training and Enterprise Council

Paula Kingston BA CertEd DipLib ALA MIInfSc
Programme Manager, National Council for Educational
Technology

Tim Lomas BA MSc ALA
Tutor Librarian, Furness College

Professor Rennie McElroy MA MBA DipLib FLA
Chief Librarian, Napier University

Margaret Oldroyd BA DipLib ALA
Staff Resources Manager, Division of Learning Development,
De Montfort University

Robert Oldroyd BA DipLib ALA
Deputy Librarian, University of Nottingham

Michael Rowarth OBE MA MEd MIPM MIMgt
Principal, Newcastle College

John Stoddart BA HonDEd CIMgt FRSA
Principal and Vice-Chancellor, Sheffield Hallam University

Ken Watson BA MEd DipLib ALA
Senior Subject Librarian, Sheffield Hallam University

Tom Wilson BSc MBCS
Principal, Glasgow College of Building and Printing

List of abbreviations

APL/A	accreditation or assessment of prior learning/achievement
BTEC	Business and Technology Education Council
CAL	computer-assisted learning
CATS	Credit Accumulation and Transfer Scheme
CBI	Confederation of British Industry
CCTV	closed-circuit television
CD-I	Compact Disc–Interactive
CD-ROM	Compact Disc–Read Only Memory
CIHE	Council for Industry and Higher Education
CLO	Circles Liaison Officer (of CoFHE)
CNAA	Council for National Academic Awards
CoFHE	Colleges of Further and Higher Education (Group of the Library Association)
COPOL	Council of Polytechnic Librarians
CPD	continuing professional development
CPVE	Certificate of Prevocational Education
CVCP	Committee of Vice-Chancellors and Principals
DES	Department of Education and Science
DFE	Department for Education
EC	European Community
EFL	English as a foreign language
FE	further education
FEFC	Further Education Funding Council
FEU	Further Education Unit
fte	full-time equivalent
GCE	General Certificate of Education
GCSE	General Certificate of Secondary Education
GNVQ	General National Vocational Qualification
HE	higher education
HEFC(E)	Higher Education Funding Council (England)
HMI	Her Majesty's Inspectorate
ILEA	Inner London Education Authority
IT	information technology
LASEC	London and South East Circle (of CoFHE)
LEA	local education authority

m²	square metres
MSC	Manpower Services Commission
NAB	National Advisory Board for Public Sector Higher Education
NATFHE	National Association of Teachers in Further and Higher Education
NCC	National Curriculum Council
NCET	National Council for Educational Technology
NCVQ	National Council for Vocational Qualifications
NJC	National Joint Council for Local Authorities' Administrative, Professional, Tecnical and Clerical Staff
NVQ	National Vocational Qualification
OPAC	Online Public Access Catalogue
OU	Open University
PC	personal computer
PCFC	Polytechnics and Colleges Funding Council
RSA	Royal Society of Arts
SCONUL	Standing Conference of National and University Libraries
SCOTCATS	Scottish Credit Accumulation and Transfer Scheme
SCOTVEC	Scottish Vocational Education Council
SEAC	Schools Examination and Assessment Council
SLIC	Scottish Library and Information Council
TEC	training and enterprise council(s)
TEED	Training, Enterprise and Education Directorate
TQM	Total Quality Management
TVEI	Technical and Vocational Education Initiative

Preface

We hope that this book may serve both as a tribute to the Colleges of Further and Higher Education (CoFHE) Group of the Library Association as it reaches its Silver Jubilee in 1994 and as a celebration of college librarianship during these 25 years. But this is not a history book. Its analytical and developmental focus directs us towards the opportunities that exist for librarians, now and in the future, to develop and support quality learning services in colleges to meet the demands of flexible and learner-centred educational provision.

Our concept of 'colleges' and therefore of 'college librarianship' embraces librarianship and related educational issues in colleges of further education, colleges of higher education and the former (i.e., pre-1992) polytechnics and Scottish central institutions. The alleged differences between the further and higher education sectors are often emphasized, but for most of the period reviewed these institutions, in both further and higher education, shared closer approaches to librarianship than did the polytechnics and the pre-1992 universities.

There is a body and a style of professional practice that can be clearly discerned and identified with these institutions. It is characterized above all by the direct involvement of librarians in educational practice and decision-making – in the classroom, in the library itself and in the board room – by its pioneering development of non-print and other non-traditional library materials, and by a willingness to put service to students and staff and exploitation of library resources before the servicing of the collections themselves (this last facilitated in part, certainly, by the relatively small size of these collections in many colleges). These features originated and were nurtured in colleges in the 1960s and early 1970s; if many of them are not now the sole preserve of college libraries, then that is testimony to the contribution that these libraries and their librarians have made to the profession at large.

The bibliographic trail is not hard to find. Several routes through the literature chart the development. One of these routes runs from the Ministry of Education in 1957,[1] the work of Gordon Wright, the 'Hertfordshire school' of college librarians[2] and the seminal research of Whitworth;[3] through early Library Association standards for college libraries[4] and the collection of essays compiled by McElroy,[5] to integrated expressions of operational policy and advice on resourcing and appraisal published in this decade by both UK and Scottish professional bodies.[6,7] The above is charted merely by way of example and to reveal something of our professional philosophical roots; many readers will identify their own trails, using partly or wholly different sets of references.

It may be unusual to feature references in a preface, but, for the record:

1   Ministry of Education, *Libraries in technical colleges*, Circular 322, Ministry of Education, 1957.

2   Wright, G. H., *The library in colleges of commerce and technology; a guide to the use of the library as an instrument of education*, Deutsch, 1966.

3   Whitworth, T. A., *The role of the technical college librarian*, Bradford University (MSc thesis), 1969.

4   For example: Library Association, *College Libraries: recommended standards of library provision in colleges of technology and other establishments of further education*, Library Association, 2nd rev. edn., 1971.

5   McElroy, A. R., (ed.), *College librarianship: the objectives and the practice*, Library Association, 1984.

6   Library Association, *Guidelines for college and polytechnic libraries*, 4th edn., Library Association, 1990.

7   Scottish Library and Information Council and Scottish Library Association, *Libraries in Scottish further education colleges; standards for performance and resourcing*, SLIC, 1993.

Throughout the period and throughout these professional developments, CoFHE and its predecessors in The Library Association's group structure have provided a professional centre for college librarians where experience could be exchanged; where people could learn from colleagues, debate with them and disagree with them; and where, through all of this, they could develop their own, and the whole sector's, concept of librarianship. CoFHE has also served as the mouthpiece for these developments and views, communicating them to The Library Association and, through it, to the educational world at large. The anecdotal evidence of professional friends and colleagues; the recorded evidence of the literature cited above and of conference proceedings, reports, articles and books too numerous to mention here; and the physical evi-

dence of the libraries themselves and their operations, suggest that
it has had some success.

Close alliance with the educational process is a key feature of
CoFHE's activity and of college librarianship itself. College librarians
have consistently involved themselves in the academic life and
debate of their institutions, contributing to academic board, learning
policy groups and – via user education – work in the classroom.
The late Keith Harris, one-time librarian of the University
of Northumbria, then Newcastle upon Tyne Polytechnic, observed
that the librarian must be seen to be effective and credible in the
institution as a whole, if s/he wished the library itself to be taken
seriously. Resources, he was wont to argue, go to people who can
be trusted to make good use of them, not to activities. To this end,
college librarians have contributed to their institutions outwith the
library, as well as within it. Following this lead from the sector of
the profession it exists to serve and stimulate, CoFHE has sought
in its courses and conferences to give its members contact with
speakers from all parts of the educational spectrum – principals,
educational technologists, open learning specialists, marketing specialists
and so on – rather than simply having librarians talk to
librarians. Colleges are complex organizations comprising many
disciplines, skills and responsibilities; college librarians do not
operate in a vacuum; it is as important to attend to the views and
visions of those who work alongside us, and manage us, as it is to
listen to our professional peers.

We had these issues in the forefront of our minds in planning
this book. By design, half of the chapters are contributed by people
who work outwith the library profession, but are in a position to
influence it. In editing the several contributions, we have been concerned
to let each writer express her/his view fully, and to let each
chapter stand on its own feet as a contribution to the literature, as
well as forming part of the whole book. Naturally, this has meant
that some topics appear in more than one chapter, since it is
impossible to discuss any one aspect of librarianship or educational
development in isolation. What is pleasing is that none of our
contributors has attempted to do so; all adopt a whole-college
approach and all exhibit a shared philosophy, amply demonstrating
the professional consensus of college librarianship.

We are grateful to our authors for giving so generously of their
time, experience and wisdom, and for tolerating the anxieties and
occasional tyranny of the editors. We thank Margaret Lynch, June

Simpson and Betty Stoddart for their help in preparing material for the press. Any faults that remain are our own.

CoFHE has provided a good professional base and network for many librarians. Our own involvements with CoFHE over some 20 years have been professionally satisfying and beneficial, personally stimulating, always enjoyable; for that, we thank colleagues whom we are privileged to call friends. We congratulate CoFHE on its silver jubilee, we commend its achievements, and we wish it a fulfilling and hectic progress towards its golden jubilee in 2019!

Marie Adams, Barnet College
Rennie McElroy, Napier University

August 1993

1

The student and the learning process

John Cowan

Introduction

In my 30 years in higher education, I have frequently found it a useful defensive ploy to describe myself, in advance of offering possibly controversial educational views, as someone whose words and views are only those of a humble engineer - a contradiction in terms, that description, if ever there was one! In the present context, and with a far from evasive motive, I wish to emphasize at the outset that I write merely from the perspective of someone who has taught in universities over the past 30 years. I make no claim to speak for the entire tertiary sector, or for the colleges in particular. I certainly have no authority in the field of librarianship. Nor am I an educational historian, one whose account of the events of the past 30 years in British tertiary education will be either comprehensive or impartial.

I write with a purpose and a partiality which I should explain briefly. My remit in this volume is to introduce some of the issues and challenges which have emerged from events in the rapidly changing world of tertiary education over the past 30 years. I am to do so in such a way that I provide a framework, and no more than that, for the writers whose contributions make up the body of the text, and whose knowledge of their specialisms is far beyond anything I can offer. In other words, I write about this subject from the perspective of 'non-librarians' who are none the less involved with this subject area - the teachers with whom librarians work, and those students whom librarians, like teachers, try to serve and support.

A 'sea change' in tertiary education

In 1960, most students in Britain were taught in a teacher-directed process, following a course structure which was defined by little more than an outline syllabus. Even the innovators who advocated and experimented with programmed learning were clearly in the business of instructing, although in their case they had espoused a doctrine which called on them to define their objectives and to communicate them explicitly to their students. What changes a mere 30 years have brought!

The emphasis has moved from teaching to learning, and to student-centred learning at that. To an ever-increasing extent, though by no means universally, students are expected to be responsible managers of at least parts of their learning, to contribute to the review of the teaching they receive, and even to share in the responsibilities of programme design. The best of teaching practice is no longer the competent provision of effective instruction; rather it is now seen as desirable to facilitate the learning and development of groups of learners whose individuality requires that they should be treated as much as possible in accordance with their distinct needs. Consequently, the demands which are currently made on those who serve in tertiary education are considerable, and challenging. For they must teach in ways which they did not experience when they themselves were learners and they must do so in the face of explicit demands for each component of the educational system to assure and to demonstrate the quality of the education which it offers. Almost without exception, departments, units and individuals are confronted by the demands of quality assessment, of quality audit and of the need to have and to operate an effective system of quality assurance. This means that, nowadays, there is much more involvement in training and staff development, more monitoring of teaching and more evaluation of the work of teachers and of the quality of courses.

All of this has occurred in a period when the available resources per student have been steadily reduced, as a result of an insistent demand to bring about efficiency gains and to reduce costs. One consequence of that has been an increased dependence on libraries and other learning resources, by those who see this as a way of cutting staff costs as well as by those who advocate independent learning for pedagogical reasons.

It should be thought provoking to look back over the process of change; to recall why and how the main developments occurred; and to reflect on the hopes of those who were responsible for them, the contrasts between aspirations and outcomes, and the issues which confront education today in consequence. I hope to initiate such reflection on the part of readers in these introductory pages.

The beginnings of revolution

In 1965, those who sought to improve tertiary education were trying to provide more effective instruction than hitherto. They specified their objectives according to Bloom's *Taxonomy of educational objectives*, or in some similar manner. They structured the instruction offered to the learner – whether in programmed learning, through various forms of personalized systems of instruction which sought to achieve mastery of material on the part of *all* learners, at *every stage*, or by carefully recording well-prepared and scripted CCTV programmes or instructional audio-tapes.

Somehow, the mood and the priorities of the innovators changed significantly in the next few years. It is tempting to suggest that this could have been inspired by the students' revolts of 1968, which had more influence in Britain than we acknowledge. On the continent they led, for example, to the so-called project-orientated courses in which the content of the students' learning was determined from the needs they realized while tackling the problems on which their learning was centred. This was in contrast to the traditional arrangement in which students are set problems which are deemed appropriate to the syllabus which their teachers have chosen for them. There were certainly those in Britain who looked with envy at the high competence of the graduates from problem-centred courses in three continents, and yearned to find a way to develop their own students' problem-solving abilities to a comparable level.

But the development of problem-centred learning was only one factor. For, by 1970, thoughtful and progressive teachers were pondering on their responses to the first version of *Freedom to learn*, by Carl Rogers – a volume which argued persuasively that the ideal teacher would facilitate learning in much the same way as client-centred therapists go about their work. There were other persuasive texts available, which made interested teachers worry about the effectiveness of lectures, and about the inability of the educational system to produce people who spotted good questions for themselves and then actively pursued the answers to these questions on their own initiative. There were a number of enthusiasts, from Postlethwaite in Purdue University to Harden in Glasgow, who had harnessed the potential of pre-recorded materials as a way of catering for individuality in learning; for planning, preparing and refining teaching; and for allowing students to work at their own speeds. Indeed, there was such a variety of innovations in tertiary and school education that the Nuffield Foundation set up a group to look into examples of independence in learning, and to publicize their best features.

There soon grew up a fellowship of those who felt that their work merited their claims to be offering 'independence' in learning. But this was a period of purely empirical development. The evaluations which were undertaken were, with few exceptions, carried out by the innovators themselves, and reported in an anecdotal manner and with sparse data. The forms of the innovatory schemes were determined and defended on intuitive grounds, and the skills inherent in the new approaches to teaching were acquired in the midst of the action.

The adjective 'independent', with its emotive overtones, was misleading. Few of the progressive teachers offered their learners much more than a measure of control over the pace of learning. Other than in project orientation, 'freedom' for the learners was still distinctly restricted.

The Open University

In 1969, the Open University (OU) came into being, and was soon to make an impact on higher education – not only in the United Kingdom, but around the world.

The OU adopted a radically different approach to higher education. It was so 'open' that it would admit any British resident of 18 years of age or older – even *much* older – without any academic qualifications whatsoever. It organized its teachers, who wrote the distance learning course materials, into course teams. These teams worked in such a way that the course philosophy and plan were approved and owned by the entire team before the detailed work of course writing began. It attached to each of these teams an educational technologist, whose role was to ensure pedagogical soundness in the courses produced. It deputed to its Institute of Educational Technology the task of evaluating courses in extensive pilot studies, in the early years of their lives, so that subsequent changes could be properly informed by actual learning outcomes. It established from the outset the principle that teaching should be appraised and monitored by colleagues. And, of particular interest, it devoted a remarkable proportion of its slight budget to the support of learners on an individual basis.

The OU had an immediate impact. This could be seen in the popularity within traditional institutions of its course texts and readers and in the use – and sometimes pillaging – of its course units and broadcast materials, which were quickly acknowledged to be of exceptional quality and effectiveness. In addition, however, those staff in existing institutions who worked part-time for the OU carried back to their own institutions the practices, standards and ideas they acquired in the OU.

The OU, however, exercised considerable control over its learners. While they had open access, and openness regarding the time and place of their studying, they still had to follow the course schedule and submit assignments according to a strict timetable. They could find and follow their own ways of learning, but few did so or were helped to do so.

Open learning

In the 1970s, though, a few innovators elsewhere were actively exploring the consequences of offering their learners control over *how* they learned, *what* they learned, and even the beginnings of some share in the process of *assessment* of their learning. In so doing, they discovered – as the OU was discovering – that independent learners had to develop, to a fairly high level, certain abilities which were not called on to any great extent when the teachers directed the learning. Learners who rejoiced in 'freedom' in their learning had to make choices, and make them wisely; they also had to monitor these choices and learn from that monitoring. These and other such demands were new, and called for programmes addressing what have generally been called study skills but were found to go far beyond the level of skills required to commence study at tertiary level.

Education for capability

Thus far, development and review had centred on the question of how students were to be taught, or how they might be taught 'better' – whatever that entails. With the publication of the *Education for capability* manifesto in 1980, the question of *what* students were taught, and, more importantly, of what they *learned* and of how they *developed*, was raised with some authority and concern. The manifesto was endorsed by an influential group of signatories drawn from industry and education. This group, who admittedly included some of the leading academics in the new area of independent learning, were convinced that education at all levels was too much concerned with the acquisition of knowledge and understanding, and too little with its use and with the development of the abilities which were inherent in that use.

They criticized in particular the concept of the 'educated person' as someone who has been neither educated nor trained to exercise useful skills, and who is able to understand but not to act. They argued powerfully the case for an education which would prepare people for a life outwith the educational system. They described that type of education in terms of four capacities which they felt were under emphasized at that time in the British educational system, in schools and beyond. These capacities were: *competence*, being the practice of skills and the use of knowledge; *coping* better with their own lives and with the problems that confront them and society; *creativity*, especially in the formulation and solution of problems and the design, manufacture and marketing of goods and services; and *cooperation* with other people and all that that entails in terms of interpersonal awareness and abilities.

Under the banner of the Royal Society of Arts, and following the enthusiastic and able leadership of people such as Charles Handy, the Education for Capability Committee set about promoting these views. Perhaps more significantly, they arranged to recognize through their awards the achievements of teachers in schools, colleges, polytechnics and universities whom they deemed to have made significant progress towards providing education for capability. Their influence, then, was twofold. They urged a radical rethinking of the nature of the curriculum, and they endorsed with some authority the work of those who had engaged with effect in the implications of such rethinking.

Once again, however, the consequent changes called in turn for radical developments in how teachers taught and in the abilities which they required in order to teach effectively towards these new goals. Those who sought to educate for capability – who included the advocates of independent learning – aspired to develop purposefully the higher-level cognitive abilities such as true creativity, rather than the imitation of someone else's creative effort; self-evaluation; and also that (genuine) analysis which goes beyond the application of standard and predictable analytical procedures. They were concerned with affective goals, which related to the nurturing and handling of values, and furthermore they had taken interpersonal goals on to their curricula, both in terms of skills and understanding of social transactions. Notice, too, that changes of this nature in *declared* curricula are pointless unless they are reflected in the hidden curricula which able students can detect in the assessment systems they are required to satisfy. Thus it was not only methods of teaching which had to change, but also methods of assessment.

Methods of assessment

The literature on assessment in higher education which was available, even in 1965, was noteworthy for the high proportion of critical and rigorous studies which had been contributed by teachers who worried about the way their own subjects were being assessed – by themselves and by their immediate colleagues. They scrutinized, and were appalled by, the unreliability of the results on which their own boards of examiners reached judgements. They also wrote, with less objectivity perhaps, about the validity of these assessments – the issue of whether or not they examined that which it was intended they should examine.

In consequence, generated from within the disciplines themselves, teachers had access to the work of small groups of concerned enthusiasts whose credentials could not be rejected by their disciplinary colleagues, and whose findings it was usually impossible to reject and simple to confirm. One or two were prompted by these findings to the point of relating the supposed acquisition of competencies during higher education to the performance of these skills in work-related contexts – with horrifying but convincing findings.

Methods of assessment were, at least nominally, established on the agenda for teachers in tertiary education, as a matter for careful consideration and informed choice and evaluation. Sadly, some 25 years later, methods of assessment still are all too often chosen without being justified on the grounds of coherent reasoning, and even in direct contravention of what is known about their appropriateness and influences on learning.

Learning outcomes

In Gothenburg, at Lancaster and Surrey universities, and in the OU, able researchers had been studying learning, as opposed to teaching. They looked into learning outcomes in familiar circumstances, albeit in situations which had often been reformulated for the purposes of enquiry. They discovered that the way we teach can have a powerful influence on the way students learn, and they also unearthed much thought-provoking and useful information about the individuality of student needs in learning situations. These researches were a great boost and source of inspiration for teachers who wished to devise situations which offered real scope for worthwhile adult learning.

The researchers published their findings in such a way that the results of their work were both comprehensible to rank-and-file teachers and authoritative. And so it came about that those who had had an intuitive belief in independent learning and in education for capability had data, concepts, and arguments which they could use in debate with colleagues who clung firmly to traditional methods, and who resisted change – even on the part of others. The move to concentrate on learning rather than teaching now had the beginnings of a popular and practical pedagogy. But in a sense 'pedagogy' is the wrong word; for I seek to convey the distinctness of adult learning, which is not the same as learning in childhood and adolescence, and requires its own concepts, principles and methods. I would prefer not to describe that, as some have done, as 'androgogy' – since that means the study of the learning of adult men! Whatever title is used, though, it is a different knowledge base about different learning which we are considering, and which teachers in tertiary education were seeking at this time. Thanks to the researchers, they now had the beginnings of a conceptual basis from which to plan and evaluate their curriculum developments.

By 1980, it was rare to take part in an institutional review of a polytechnic and to enquire about its thinking in response to recent researches on student learning without encountering at least some who could tell of innovations which had stemmed from their reactions to the Gothenburg work, or to the writings of Entwistle and Hounsell, or of Gibbs. Nevertheless, the work which was published and generally available to teachers at that time was informative about what was going wrong in respect of student learning rather than offering proven suggestions about how to bring about improvements.

The Council for National Academic Awards

At this point it is important to identify and acknowledge the creative influence of the Council for National Academic Awards (CNAA) over the post-war period. This body was charged with maintaining academic standards in those polytechnics and colleges whose courses it was prepared to recognize, by awarding their graduates CNAA degrees. That oversight took two main forms – course approval and institutional review. Both involved visits by peers, chosen from other public sector institutions, from the universities and from industry.

About 1980, CNAA enlarged their cadre of specialist advisers in teaching, learning and assessment, and encouraged them to take more initiative in pursuing those areas of academic concern during institutional reviews. These specialists met regularly, to determine priorities for the group as a whole. At one such meeting, for example, they decided to stress the question of student learning, and to encourage institutions to find ways of informing themselves about the nature of the immediate learning which was a consequence of the teaching, so that they might review and revise that teaching accordingly.

Inevitably, the efforts of CNAA and its specialist advisers encouraged the discussion, dissemination and often the extension of good practice in teaching and assessment. Innovators were expected to table their evaluative findings in a way which would convince externals visiting an institution; this often meant that their colleagues in other departments and faculties learned for the first time what was going on in their own institution, and were able to make their own judgements about the usefulness and desirability of these developments for their own courses and departments. Teaching and learning concerns were now items on formal agendas. Teachers collected and appraised data about the acceptability of at least some aspects of educational practice. Some worried about the shallowness of the way this was being done and some reacted constructively by setting out to find ways to inform the processes of judgement more usefully, with meaningful indicators describing valid learning outcomes.

The CNAA in general, and its committee for institutions in particular, stressed the need for quality assurance to be a concern for the entire institution and for ownership of that responsibility to be vested in the entire staff group. As polytechnics moved towards accredited status with CNAA - in which they were almost autonomous - and as they aspired to become universities, the demonstration of that corporate involvement in quality assurance became an important factor in the judgements made about them.

By the mid-1980s, it was apparent that the polytechnics would soon have degree-granting status in some form or another, and that the standards which they were now setting and the ways in which they were assuring quality would establish norms to which universities and colleges would have to aspire.

Aspects of quality

The CNAA had looked for structures for quality assurance within institutions, long before much thought had been given to BS5750 or to Total Quality Management (TQM) or other formal management styles. The council expected institutions to have systems in place which would assure the quality of courses and teaching *before* they were delivered, by anticipating and eliminating weaknesses. They should also review the outcomes, not just to pick up problems within some quality control mechanism, but to ensure that such mechanisms were functioning adequately and to reorganize institutional practices and structures if and when these permitted weak provision to obtain approval under existing quality assurance procedures. And there should be a general commitment at the grass roots to the pursuit of quality in educational provision, through quality assurance procedures.

The Committee of Vice-Chancellors and Principals (CVCP) responded to this public sector norm in the late 1980s, by establishing for the traditional universities and the OU the Academic Audit Unit. This was soon to become the Division for Quality Audit of the Higher Education Quality Council, and would apply to all autonomous degree-granting institutions, once the binary line had been removed.

In some ways audit has seemed almost to leapfrog over the process of external judgement, albeit by peers, and to replace it with the more sophisticated concept of *self*-appraisal; for audit of an individual university, technically at least, takes place at the request of a vice-chancellor to an organization which the vice-chancellors themselves set up, on their own initiative. This invitation is remitted to a group of three auditors under the supervision of an assistant director of the unit, together with an audit secretary. They are given a summary of how the institution assures quality in the educational part of its operations, together with examples of that practice which are supplied to, or later requested by, the auditors to illustrate the process in action. The auditors are then asked to confirm or otherwise the effectiveness and comprehensiveness of the procedures which are in place. Where they find discrepancies or omissions, they report these in factual terms. It is not within their remit or their procedures to make judgements, other than to commend examples of good or innovative practice or to suggest aspects of the quality assurance mechanisms and structures to which the institution may wish to give further attention.

Quality Audit, in the first three years of its auditing activity, only visited what were then known as the 'traditional' universities. During these three years, and in the period which immediately preceded them, most of these universities had devoted considerable effort to establishing or developing procedures for quality assurance, which had hitherto been conspicuous by their absence. The best of the developments which ensued or which were consolidated were commendable and constructive. The traditional universities did not blindly follow CNAA and the public sector, but often established their own individualistic structures. In particular, since the initiatives began and were led from within, some devoted useful thought to the criteria against which their judgements of quality should be made.

Hard on the heels of Quality Audit and the demise of CNAA came the announcement that the new funding councils in England, Wales and Scotland would be charged with assessing the quality of the education provided by individual departments within institutions. They were to use these assessments in deciding on the number of funded places in the future (and in the long term) and, probably, the level of funding for these places. At first it seemed likely that assessments would be external, albeit peer, judgements. Quickly, the several funding councils, in different ways and at different paces, moved to the position of beginning the process of assessment from self-assessments produced by the departments under scrutiny.

The three funding councils then proceeded rather differently. For our present purpose, however, it is noteworthy that they have all emphasized that they are interested in outcome judgements rather than judgements of input. In other words, it is not the quality of teaching which should be predominant in assessments, but the quality of the learning and of the learning experiences which that teaching generates. They invite institutions to consider the performance indicators which should be used as the basis for ingathering the data against which the assessment should be made. Interestingly, they also specify that assessments should be made in the context of the declared mission statement of the institution.

Hence an institution, or rather a particular department within it, is asked to declare what it is trying to achieve educationally for students in a particular discipline, how it judges its success in so doing, and what judgement it has formulated on that basis. It then rests with the team of assessors to decide if they are convinced by the evidence presented and subsequently ingathered during their visit to the institution, *if* they decide to make a visit. (Here, incidentally, there are interesting differences already in the procedures of the three councils.)

Unlike quality audit, quality assessment is an external requirement. It cannot be avoided unless an institution feels able to proceed without funding provided by government. There are ongoing, at the time of writing, debates about the amount and duplication of effort involved in the two processes; later they will no doubt be refined and streamlined, if not amalgamated. However, it does not seem profitable to speculate about the way oversight of educational quality and of the structures for assuring it may proceed, nor to explore in this chapter the differences in arrangements between higher education and further education. What is noteworthy is the creation of a situation with several new features, as far as all teachers in tertiary education are concerned. These new factors are that funding will be related to assessments of teaching quality, that these judgements will be made public and so will also affect enquiries and recruitment, that criteria against which teaching will be judged are to be made explicit and a subject for ongoing dialogue and debate, and that these judgements will concentrate on learning rather than on the teaching which leads to that learning.

At a conference in 1992, I heard an official speaker from a traditional university volunteer the information that 'At the moment, the only documentation for some of our courses is the course title.' The point of the anecdote is not the vagueness of that situation, but the fact that the university had seen fit to appoint a senior member of staff to bring about a rapid change which would eliminate that vagueness.

Small wonder that I wrote earlier of a sea change in British tertiary education. Thirty years ago the only judgements of quality in education at the tertiary level were made by Her Majesty's Inspectorate (HMI) and did not extend to the universities. These judgements were based on the teaching on offer. The criteria were far from explicit. Only a minority of institutions had structures in place to take responsibility for quality and such structures as were in existence usually concentrated on quality control, with the prompt identification and rectifying of defects in the educational provision.

Access and mobility

Throughout almost all of the period of which I write, there has been encouragement, at first from outwith the educational establishments themselves, for a more flexible system of tertiary education. The desire was to make it more possible for more students to enter further education and higher education, and to progress through it successfully and to the limits of their potential. There should be entry routes for students without traditional qualifications, and preparatory courses of some kind to enable those who did not quite meet the formal entry requirements to top up their qualifications. There should be structures which would enable students to transfer between courses according to their preferences, and to respond to their changing interests and to performances different from those predicted from their entry qualifications. It should be possible to study part-time, or at a distance.

By 1985, most institutions had come to perceive development and economic effectiveness in terms of flexibility of provision, and of expansion. They were therefore usually keen to take up offers of funding to provide access courses and they had begun to adjust their course structures to permit students to build up a profile of attainment which stemmed from their interests and aspirations, and reflected their abilities, and to study in a variety of modes. Nationally, CNAA took the lead in encouraging the scheme for Credit Accumulation and Transfer (CATS) which, in theory at least, made it possible to obtain a degree with courses taken from more than one institution. A similar development occurred in Scotland, with the title SCOTCATS. Neither scheme led to much interchange of students between institutions, other than as a form of higher level 'access' in which students who began their studies in a college working for a certificate or a diploma might move on to degree-level work at a university or polytechnic. Hence, the accumulation of credit became more a matter for accumulation within institutions whose course structures had hitherto been more compartmentalized and constraining. The transfer of credit in such situations brought unobtrusively on to the agenda the issues associated with the comparability and credibility of credit.

Many course structures were idiosyncratic, and built up from interlocking components of varying magnitudes and inter-relationships. Quite apart from the timetabling difficulties which this placed in the way of those who sought a more flexible design of qualification by 'picking and mixing' the provision on offer, departments which were willing to allow students to accumulate credit with them faced great difficulties in working out how to integrate, in their assessment schemes, components of differing shapes and sizes, taken from different sources.

For these and other reasons, the move towards modularization of courses has proceeded apace. More and more institutions assemble course provision in units of one or more standard magnitudes, and with defined levels which indicate the standard of achievement demanded of the learner. Further, it has become common for such modules to be clearly defined in terms of content and learning outcomes, so that those who monitor and approve courses based on accumulation of credit can check readily that there has been no duplication of credit and that the prerequisites for certain subsequent study have indeed been covered by a given learner.

Here, then, without direct external intervention or initiative (as in the case of quality assessment), we had another pressure calling on teachers to define what learners learn and to what standard.

Resourcing

Resources for education, in real terms and measured as resource per student, have been steadily reduced in recent years. This has been described as a requirement to bring about efficiency gains. It is fair to admit that some educational practices in the past were far from cost-effective; there can be few valid reasons for regretting the way these have been trimmed, if not eliminated, by the reduction in resources. Nevertheless, it is equally realistic to point out that many services which were available to students in the past have been reduced or have disappeared. There are fewer tutorials, and those which occur involve larger student groups. There is a greater delay in marking and returning assignments. There is more exploitation of self-study methods and materials, more emphasis on small groups operating without tutors, and more self-assessment by students.

Not all of these changes have been made to enhance the quality of learning. Neither are all of them undesirable. Some have allowed innovators to pursue – with economic benefits which management has welcomed – initiatives, such as self-assessment, which these enthusiasts have advocated for some years on pedagogical grounds. Whatever the reasons, the pattern of learning activities on offer and the nature of the learners' experiences of teaching are still changing markedly.

Pedagogical progress

The teacher in 1980 could read the published work of the researchers from Gothenburg and elsewhere, and be stimulated to wonder how to respond to the weaknesses in learning and teaching which they highlighted. Today's teachers are in a much more fortunate position, for educationists such as Entwistle, Ramsden and Gibbs have helpfully followed through their earlier work. They have now been able to address the need to offer concepts, methods and examples which can be taken up by serving teachers who have no training as educational researchers, and no opportunity to engage in front-line educational development.

There are now available many instruments which enable teachers and students to explore learning styles and the impact of differing teaching-learning strategies on the nature of learning. There are well-documented examples, taken from a range of disciplines, in which new methods of teaching and learning have been thoroughly planned and properly evaluated. The data available illuminate the conclusions and recommendations of these evaluations, and makes the content of the case studies potentially useful in a cross-disciplinary way.

There are also a number of courses for teachers available nowadays which go far beyond the tentative and frequently ineffective staff development programmes of 30 years ago. Teachers can gain certification for studies and achievements in the teaching of their own subject. They are encouraged to become reflective practitioners, following the work of Schon and taking up an ongoing and enquiring responsibility for the quality and development of the teaching which they offer. The concept of the teachers as action researchers of their own practice in the field of adult learning is still in its infancy, but steadily growing to maturity. And many institutions now have awards which internally reflect the values of such national schemes as the Partnership Awards, which recognize and reward effective teaching.

The changes – and the challenges which they bring with them

The greatest change, which has run like a thread of scarlet through my account of these 30 years, is the shift from systems and situations which concentrated on teaching to those which concentrate on learning. Nowadays, we pass responsibility to students to manage their learning, for various reasons. We recognize their individuality as learners, and we try to cope with that by making learning

something which is less standardized, and hence more student centred. We accept that it is learning and the learning experience
which are the outcomes of our labours, and on which we should
judge the value of our efforts and in turn be judged by those who
provide us with resources.

The challenge which confronts us all as a result of this change is
to find out more about how our students learn; more about how
well they have learned, and what the learning experience has
involved for them; more about the relationship between the assessment methods and demands, and the learning which they encourage and identify. We should then use all of that information to
enable us to design, detail, deliver and evaluate more effective and
efficient teaching and learning situations. Too long has the phrase
'teaching and learning' been used glibly, when the speakers or writers meant merely 'teaching' - and instruction at that. Our challenge is to be involved effectively with all aspects of the teaching
and learning relationship, and to see teaching - dare I suggest it -
as the purposeful creation of situations from which motivated
learners should not be able to escape without significantly learning
or developing as a result of our efforts. That definition covers
instruction - aye, *and* facilitation and student support in all forms
and places, *including libraries and information centres.*

Student-centred learning is by its very nature individualized. To
be feasible, let alone economic, it must therefore involve much
study which is independent - in the sense that it is not constantly
supported or directed by a teacher, even if the teacher is facilitative.
This is necessarily more demanding for the student - partly because
more is expected of the learner in directing and monitoring learning and partly because syllabus changes over these three decades
have brought a shift in levels and domains, so that course goals are
of themselves more demanding than hitherto. Consequently, learners need more effective support, and teachers need more sophisticated skills, to be used efficiently in supporting ever-growing numbers
of students with ever-diminishing resources. Here, the librarians are
in the forefront of the battle to assure quality in education. It is in
and from libraries and information centres that students increasingly study. It is the staff there who are confronted with any inadequa-
cies, in material resources and - more importantly - in student competencies. It is often librarians who find themselves providing remedial tuition and then setting up initial training in study skills so
that such remedial demands can be lessened.

When we teachers (and my liberal definition includes librarians in that category) decide, for whatever reasons, upon a learning environment which assumes that a significant proportion of the learning will be self-managed, and independent in that sense, then we have challenged ourselves to equip our students with the abilities which they require in that situation. We have to develop not merely the simple initial skills, but also the more sophisticated competencies such as decision-making and decision-monitoring, such as the noticing and defining of worthwhile questions and problems, as well as the answering of the questions implicit in these problems. Our challenge is to find, develop and evaluate formatively the methods of teaching and student support which will be effective in meeting such needs, and which should even lead to deeper and more valuable learning than did the old instructional regimes.

Evaluation, of course, can have many forms and purposes. I have assumed in much of what I have written that we should build on the potential of those styles of evaluation which are 'illuminative'. They yield data which are essentially value free, save in the choice of the areas from which they have been collected; those data then 'illuminate' the nature of the teaching and learning situation as it is, and assist those involved and responsible for the teaching to consider where and how improvements may be possible, and what features should be retained and enhanced.

That, in turn, presupposes that we engage with formative evaluation in the first instance; that we are concerned to form and reform the education, learning from mistakes and weaknesses, and striving to bring about improvements. Nevertheless, the world, before our seemingly endless attempts to get things right, demands that summative evaluations are made. We must nowadays contribute to, or even provide, quality judgements about the value of the education which we have provided. If we do not do so, others will make such judgements on their own, and we may regret the outcomes!

The challenge in this case we have already explored at some length. It is to find meaningful and useful ways of measuring learning *outcomes* and to find qualitative ways of describing and comparing learning *experiences*. We have a long way to go in response to this challenge. Whatever the rhetoric of the funding councils, the reality is that the performance indicators they suggest and use currently are almost entirely of inputs or are distinctly superficial measures of learning output.

The greater involvement of students is an attractive notion. At first sight it seems an obvious improvement to ingather feedback from them, to set up consultative committees and to let students contribute to course evaluations. Nevertheless, the evidence from audits and elsewhere suggests that students are not always keen to take up these opportunities, find them sometimes ineffective, have difficulty contributing to discussions where they have little of the background information and only slight and particular educational experience, and feel that their contributions have little influence and are usually outvoted – except where they describe straightforward failures by the system to provide what it promised to provide.

It is arguable that students who share in the responsibility for important educational decisions should be as trained and competent to do so as are the teachers engaged with the same task and that, since they clearly bring a different experience and motive to the process of consultation and providing and using feedback, their role in such participation also needs to be more clearly worked out. Our challenge in this area, then, is to identify what we expect of students and to prepare them to do that competently and effectively.

Most important of all, we have moved to a situation which is rapidly developing and will continue to develop, where teachers will be constantly expected to plan, programme, deliver and evaluate the teaching and learning situations for which they are responsible, and where they will increasingly be held accountable, *by* their institutions and *on behalf* of their institutions, for the quality and soundness of what they provide. Teaching in tertiary education in five years' time will undoubtedly not be the same as teaching today.

We are thus challenged to engage with the ongoing process of development and review in a thoroughly professional manner, and to be accountable for the ways in which we do so.

Professionalism

The business of higher and further education must be professional in its methods, demands and staffing. I take a profession, such as that of medicine or engineering, to be a field of study and practice in which there is a hard core of specialized knowledge that is well substantiated; where that core of professional knowledge is used by most professionals on most occasions as the basis upon which they reach the decisions about the actions which their professional engagement demands of them – decisions that, in the main, should be similar, whichever professional arrives at them. Certainly, that is the expectation I would have of a representative of the medical profession who might attend me in a severe illness. And it is what I believe the general public are entitled to expect of their engineers, who design buildings and machinery and plant, where professional incompetence can readily lead to injury or loss of life, for members of the general public.

According to that interpretation, I judge that librarians are already professionals, but that tertiary teachers, in the main, are not. I strongly suggest that tertiary teachers must become professional in their work with learners as soon as possible, and that in the interim they should give heed to those in their midst, such as librarians, who have relevant professional competence to contribute.

The place of libraries and librarianship

In the most radical of tertiary institutions, the greatest changes I observe are those which involve libraries and librarians. I have visited institutions where the 'library' has genuinely become the 'library and information service'. The induction of new arrivals in basic study skills is a responsibility of that service and the ongoing responsibility for the continuing development of many of the competencies which are central to the students' curricula is taken up by them. They see it as a commitment in which they can and should play a dominant role. Consequently, we can now point to a number of noteworthy developments in institutions where the focus for educational research and development, as it affects student learning and the support of that learning, is located in the extended library and its staff.

Surely this is just as it should be? For decades, educational librarians have been trained to obtain, use and apply information on behalf of enquirers from a wide assortment of disciplines. They have been expected to acquire and use the abilities to enable them to do so. They have often researched in this very field. It seems logical that they should now be at the forefront of the developments taking place in supporting student-centred learning, which has been the (somewhat neglected) function and competence of university and college librarians since time immemorial. The neglect, I hasten to add, seems to have been on the part of the institutions and not the librarians!

That is why the contributions which librarians and others now make in this volume, describing their responses to the developments and the challenges I have outlined, are of significance and value to education as a whole, as well as to librarians in particular.

2

The institutional context: further education

Michael Rowarth

Remember the days when libraries were small rooms guarded by fierce ladies? The Holy Grail in those far-off days was to have a library in which the books never left the shelves, never mind the library, and if students did dare to penetrate the portals, they were to remain in silence. In those days, the low image of libraries and the consequent low morale of library staff emanated from a lack of location within the old technical college ethos. Universities and schools had libraries – they were a sign of academic respectability – but technical colleges, having been given libraries by an architect or an education committee, had some difficulty in knowing what to do with them. In the beginning, to quote a phrase, technical colleges had been – in perception if not in fact – peopled by construction and engineering apprentices. Their interest in libraries was perceived as being scant. The library became the alternative classroom for the general studies class.

These were the (relatively recent) dark ages. The dawn has come gradually and from different points of the compass. Some colleges have seen a statistical discrepancy between what the former Department of Education and Science (DES) – now the Department For Education (DFE) – norms, based on square metres (m^2) per student, entitle them to in terms of library space and what they actually have. Others have begun to see that the role of the library has been vastly under-rated and that something must be done. It has to be said, however, that other colleges have seen nothing until financial levers have pulled their libraries out of obscurity.

However they have reached their current position, colleges are now faced with the need to provide a service which their original library bases are ill-equipped to deliver. Newcastle College is such a college. It will not be typical, because the starting points of individual colleges vary enormously, but what follows will show how one college has come to address the local and national demands for change. As such, it will reflect, in part, the experience of other institutions.

To start at the very beginning is to recognize a small library of 698m^2 with capacity for 96 students, but with 4,339 full-time equivalent (fte) students in the college. It was staffed with three library staff, three clerks and four part-time clerical staff; its book stock was 60,000 volumes and the budget was £22,552. Separately, there was within the college an education technology unit, providing audiovisual resources for teaching purposes. The library service had little or no prestige in the institution. Its relevance was questionable and it was consequently under-resourced. A change of attitude was required if there was to be any development.

That change came with the appointment of a vice-principal to take responsibility for academic affairs whose experience was of the higher education sector. To him, the library's insignificance stood out like a sore thumb and he set about doing something about it. The first task was to look at the size of the institution, the size of the library and the general recommendations of Her Majestry's Inspectorate (HMI) regarding the ratio of students to library capacity. The library was less than half the size it should have been.

The first step in bringing about change, therefore, was a realization of the problem by someone at a sufficiently high level in the organization; that is, at a level which commanded enough clout to get things done.

The second step was to solve the problem! The initial identification of the problem opened the college's eyes to the fact that the library service was fundamental to the learning of many of the college students. The college, without anybody having overtly recognized it, was not an old-fashioned technical college any longer. It had a majority of business studies and GCE students. The library was no longer the subject of a simple visit with a tutor to explain its existence; it was becoming much more important. But it still occupied the same lowly place in the organization that it had occupied for many years: it was almost an afterthought – certainly not central to the thinking and the academic life of the organization, and with no place round decision-making tables. And that is where the breakthrough occurred.

The college upgraded the library service to the equivalent of a mainstream department. It was not just a question of importance: it was a question of image too. If the strongest of signals had not gone out to say that the library service was vital to the life of the college, the college community would still have treated it as second class. An advertisement appeared, therefore, for a head of library graded as a head of an academic department. The response was, as you would expect, dramatic. That was the visible start. The invisible start was a desire on the part of top management to solve the problem fundamentally, not superficially. It was of no value to make an appointment without financial back-up, and without a willingness to take a risk by giving the new head as free a hand as possible.

At the same time as recruitment of a head of library services was taking place, plans were approved by the governing body, the local education authority (LEA) and the DES for a library extension.

So the college came to the point where it had a new library head, the existing library staff, an old one-room library and an agreement for a new library extension. The head set to work with a vengeance and at its completion the new library struck us all between the eyes. It was visually startling, colourful and attractively laid out with, for those early days, such unimaginable furnishings as carpets and easy chairs. It was an immediate success.

The success was not, of course, because of the visual impact. The staff had changed too - not in personnel, but in attitude. They responded positively to the new recognition of their value and to the stimulus of a new, enthusiastic and creative manager. As the library staff became more proactive so the students and the lecturing staff began to use the service more. As the usage figures grew, so the need for more staff and stock became evident. The demands for increasing funding tested college management's commitment and they responded - never as well as the library service would have wished, of course, but they responded.

The next step was a rationalization of the college's educational services. An educational technology service had grown up within a department of general studies; it provided the audiovisual equipment for lecturing staff at a fairly basic, but adequate, level. The library service and the educational technology service were natural bedfellows and a marriage was arranged without too much organizational pain.

To recap, what had happened within the college up to this point was a recognition that the function of the library had been vastly under-rated and, consequently, under-resourced. The college had recognized that a radical, root-and-branch approach to the problem was necessary. It had accordingly made a dramatic move by treating the library service as a highly graded academic department and staffing it accordingly, with leadership at head of department level.

It had created a new library extension. But, most important of all, it had taken risks by being willing to give the new head a free rein. To be brutal, however, all that had happened was that the library service had become what it always should have been. It was not a change of kind, but of degree. The scene was now set for that change in kind - a change from passive to active, from being part of the teaching strategy to part of the learning strategy.

Let us stand back for a moment, so that the movement of the library from the wings to the centre of the stage can be seen against the background of movement across the curriculum formulation and delivery front as a whole. Further education colleges had never been required, historically, to have a curriculum strategy. Indeed the very phrase 'curriculum strategy' would have caused some bewilderment in past years as to what could possibly be meant. External examinations were the order of the day, via City and Guilds, the Royal Society of Arts (RSA), GCE examining boards and a plethora of professional examining bodies. Normally, the nearest colleges got to creating further education curricula on a national scale were some Ordinary National Certificate and Diploma examinations, Mode 3 GCE examinations and, on a local scale, involvement in the work of regional examining bodies. Colleges were fed - and were happy to be fed - with the external spoon; they had known little else. Then in the 1970s came the Business Education Council and the Technician Education Council which began opening up the colleges' influence on the curriculum. The two organizations merged into what is now called the Business and Technology Education Council (BTEC). Under BTEC, colleges create their own curricula within the rules laid down, subject to the scrutiny of moderators.

At the same time as BTEC was developing, in 1977, the Further Education Unit (FEU) was created with a specific remit for the curriculum and its development. The influence of the FEU has been more far reaching than is at first apparent. It has sought to stimulate colleges on curriculum matters in a variety of forms: on the one hand, through regular reports on curricular issues, ranging from provision for people with disabilities and learning difficulties, to the implications of key technologies in education; on the other hand, by seminars and through FEU regional staff acting as curriculum catalysts. It has endeavoured to share good practice, to articulate the curriculum links between various sectors - especially between schools and further education, and to influence the major

national players on the curriculum front, including Schools
Examination and Assessment Council (SEAC), the National Curriculum
Council (NCC) and the National Council for Vocational
Qualifications (NCVQ). At a time when colleges have been concerned
more about management than curriculum, it has provided a
timely and persistent reminder of why colleges exist, asking pertinent
questions about their learning and teaching strategies.

In addition to BTEC and the FEU, there have been in the turbulent
period of the 1980s a number of other major influences on
the curriculum and on learning and teaching strategies. Open
and/or distance learning has been one. It has stemmed essentially
from three sources: one is the success of the Open University
(OU); another is the (incorrect) perception that it is cheaper than
conventional learning; the last is the insatiable desire of educationists
to experiment. These three strands have manifested themselves
in the Open Tech Unit, a creature of the Manpower Services
Commission (MSC) which consumed much resource, produced
comparatively little, but had the beneficial effect of breaking the
mould of traditional thinking. The Open Tech Unit is now transmuted
into a series of open learning networks. It would be fair to
say that open or distance learning has never captured a large share
of the traditional market, but it has found a place in colleges, providing
another arrow in the delivery quiver.

A further major national influence on the further education curriculum
scene is the NCVQ. It was created in 1987 with a remit to
achieve a coherent national framework for vocational qualifications
in England, Wales and Northern Ireland. It has been slow to
deliver, but its task has been gargantuan, even without the political
intrigue and obduracy of vested interests. A major impact of
NCVQ has been the vesting of power in individual industry-led
bodies, rather than in the traditional examining and validating
organizations. They have produced, under Department of
Employment supervision, a competence-based, modular curriculum
model, linked with realistic work environments, which will
dramatically alter the face of further education.

There is another influence which, as yet, has touched further
education only fleetingly. This is the accreditation of current and
prior learning (APL), whereby previous and current experience can
be assessed and verified and be counted as credit towards an academic
award. In the ultimate situation, APL can result in the award
of a qualification without the candidate having attended a course.

In most cases, however, there will still be gaps to be filled in by curriculum offerings.

The final national influence (sometimes curriculum-related, sometimes not) is access. There has been, over the past decade at least, a growing emphasis on access, often related to the specific markets of women, the disabled and ethnic minorities. It has been access at either end of further education – that is, easing entry into college at one end and opening up entry to the erstwhile polytechnics (and, more recently, to traditional universities) at the other. In its reverse manifestation of franchising, this movement has had specific curriculum impact, although it may have been spurred as much by the lower costs of further education institutions as by any particular educational philosophy.

The above influences are directly curriculum-related and have major implications for the curriculum and for the library service. There is another influence which is not directly curriculum-related, but which will have the greatest impact of all – that is, the unit of resource. So far, the relationship between funding and curriculum has been somewhat tenuous. Finance has been the remit of the local authority and whilst local authority budgets have been reducing, the reflection of reductions on the curriculum and its delivery has been, generally speaking, accidental and reactive. With the arrival of the Further Education Funding Council (FEFC) and a national thrust for a reduction in the unit of resource over education as a whole, curricula and their delivery will begin to be finance driven.

Overarching all of these influences have been a number of themes, all of which are affecting the library service. The first theme is the marketing of further education, which, after the 1985 Audit Commission report, has placed an ever-increasing demand on an ever-reducing budget. The result of this drive for a profitable marketing approach has shown itself in many ways, but especially in the upgrading of the physical environment.

Second of the overarching themes is quality. Quality has been launched strongly across the nation and it is having its effect in further education, on all its operations, but especially in the areas of curriculum, teaching and learning strategies, and student support services.

The final overarching theme is technology. The sector has come a long way from the programmed learning machines of the 1960s; the highly sophisticated computerized equipment now available has been, and is continuing to be, a major influence on curricula and on learning methods.

This brief overview of the major movements in the curriculum, the strategy and environment for its delivery and the financing of that delivery, is essential background to our understanding of the developing library.

So let us return to our library service, now integrated with educational technology and poised on the edge of this new and perhaps rather frightening world. It faces the waves of influence referred to above as a fully blown department of the college, part of the college's planning processes, both inside and outside the academic board, and playing its particular part in decision-making which becomes ever more critical.

We begin with the modular curriculum. NCVQ are demanding a modular approach. It makes sense for those who wish to accumulate their credits at a pace they dictate themselves. It makes sense for those who cannot attend a full course. It makes sense for those who, having gone through an APL process, then find themselves with gaps in their knowledge which need to be filled before qualifications can be awarded. It has all the hall-marks of a user-friendly, access-driven, customer-orientated approach!

What are the practical implications of this approach? First of all, let us not underestimate the size of the problem, which is huge. It has to be recognized that this is the inexorable direction of further education; it will not change in the foreseeable future and there is no virtue in pretending otherwise. So let us look the problem squarely in the face.

We need to understand that it will be totally impossible for colleges to cope with this modular approach by adopting conventional teaching strategies. Self-study through learning packages will be an imperative part of the process if this flexible, modular approach is to work.

So, then, where are the packages for self-study which will be required at some stage in the students' experience? Some do exist already, but not in anything like the quantity required, and certainly not necessarily matching the precise requirements of a National Vocational Qualification (NVQ) module.

The first problem is creating the packages. Before you can create the packages, however, you have to create an environment that stimulates production. That can be achieved by providing sufficient money to commission external agencies to write the packages, or by providing sufficient money to enable the packages to be written internally or by a consortium of colleges. Both approaches cost – and at a high rate. Both have both an up-side and a down-side. The external commission can require so much briefing, editing and general supervision that the college may well feel it has almost done the job itself. On the other hand, internal production does not start from a pool of staff with the ability to write packages (an art in itself), nor does it have the conditions in which they can be produced easily.

So, if a college decides to write its own packages, how does it set about creating the necessary conditions?

First, it has to recognize that package writing is not the God-given expertise of every member of the academic staff. One part of the exercise, therefore, must be to provide opportunity for the development of that expertise. This can be taken account of via the normal staff development procedures, although the scale of the operation will make heavy demands on funding. That first step is fairly straightforward and does not cause any trauma. It is critically important, however, that in that staff development programme the specification for a college package is clearly laid down, so that, when staff come to write packages for use by students, they follow a specific format and design. If that is not firmly established right at the start, individual staff members and departments will quite naturally do their own thing. Achieving standardization retrospectively will be a complicated and expensive unpicking and reassembling exercise.

Having trained those who would appear to be the appropriate staff, the college can hardly expect them to embark on a major programme of package writing in their spare time. Nor, if it really means business, can it expect the production programme to make significant progress if it is done on a little remission of timetable here and there. There has to be a root-and-branch approach via change in conditions of service. The argument goes like this: staff need substantial time if there is to be substantial output; substantial time must mean allocating at least part of student contact time; the time thus given up will be paid for by upfront, pump-priming money, which will be repaid by students in self-study situations being supervised by fewer staff than would have been the case if those same students had been in a normal classroom situation. The recognition of student contact time being equated with package production time provides the environment for production, but it does not guarantee production. That can only happen if the concept of student-centred learning has been accepted and owned by the college, especially by the management of the college. It is pointless pursuing the idea if that is not the case, for it will be doomed to failure.

So we now have staff developing packages according to agreed criteria, with the full support of management. How are they produced? Do they go into the normal administrative processes? If so, that will be likely to cause tension, since there will be competing demands on administrative staff which will be difficult for them to cope with. A better solution, which Newcastle College has adopted, is for there to be an entirely separate unit with, for example, word-processing staff and illustrators whose sole function is to produce packages. In that way, the process can be better controlled and the key importance of the modular/package thrust is recognized. The message of the totally dedicated unit will not be lost on the organization.

The next stage is establishing how the packages will be used. There are a number of clear requirements: first, students in further education will not necessarily be able to pursue private study in the same way as higher education students. They will need to refer to staff for help and advice, so it will be necessary for academic staff to be available. It would be counter-productive if those staff were in the same ratio to students as in a normal classroom or workshop situation, or if those staff had to be experts in the range of subjects covered by all the learning packages. The supervising staff are essentially to provide first-line help; students may need to refer to subject specialists later.

Secondly, both staff and students will need training in how to manage the new environment. On the whole, staff will have been used to being the fount of all wisdom, lecturing from the front of the class. They will not necessarily find it easy to be enablers, catalysts, managers of learning situations. As for the students, many of them will have been used to spoon-feeding, dependent on others rather than themselves; they will need coping skills too.

Thirdly, the administrative processes will need to adapt to accommodate a different registration system.

Fourthly, existing classrooms will not be adequate. They are unlikely to be big enough to accommodate the large groups of students necessary to effect the economies of scale required to deliver a modularized programme and, therefore, will have to be enlarged to take, say, 50–100 students. Nor will they be attractive enough to do justice to the launch of a major new approach to learning. So, much alteration and refurbishment work will need to be done.

Fifthly, those student-centred learning areas need to be managed. It needs to be clearly understood who is responsible for maintaining them, cataloguing the packages and providing staff who will work full-time in them, because the academic staff will have other duties elsewhere and cannot therefore be held accountable. Clearly, the library service (or 'learning resources' as it is now renamed) has to be responsible for both the areas and the staff. These areas are, in practice, extensions of the library, demanding similar resources in terms of staffing and management and much the same expertise as the normal college library.

If we pause for a moment we can see that the old, one-room library has sunk without trace. Its new name of learning resources is more than just a change of name: it is a change of philosophy and attitude. That is further reflected quantitatively in the massive increase in space, seating capacity having increased from 96 to 810 and area from 698m² to 2,560m². Staffing has increased from 16 to 51 and includes curriculum information officers in the new student-centred learning areas, production staff for packages, staffing for the whole print operation for the college and the media services, providing education technology. The budget has risen from £22,552 in 1981-2 to £357,000 in 1992-3. Some of those changes are due to an increase in students, but most of them are due to the new thrust, anticipating the effects of modularization of the curriculum.

It can be seen therefore that learning resources, which moved from the wings on to the stage, is now beginning to take a position centre stage, justifying the original decision to equate the library service with that of the academic departments.

Let us make no mistake about the significance and importance of what we are doing and the wish associated with it. It is a quantum leap that we are in the process of executing. How do we make sure we don't fall flat on our faces? In essence, we need to be sure we are managing it, that it is not controlling us. To manage it effectively, we need to be convinced that it is the right strategy, and in the continual change now characteristic of further education we should be returning constantly to first principles to confirm our strategy. Does the future indicate that the right lines are being pursued? Who can predict? We do have some pointers.

First, no change is anticipated in the national drive for the unit of resource in the further education sector to go down. Nor is a change expected in the policy that students in further education will increase, in order to help the national effort to raise skill and qualification levels, so that we can compete more effectively internationally. We shall, in other words, be expected to do more with less. We should, therefore, take note of Sir Christopher Ball: 'More means different.' The traditional teaching model cannot be sustained. That would seem to be a certainty and would thus confirm the strategy.

The second confirmation comes from the drive towards output-related funding. Education has been essentially process rather than product orientated, but the national thrust is to reverse that situation. This can be seen especially in the Department of Employment, which funds training and enterprise councils (TECs) on that basis and thus forces colleges down that route. Colleges are further affected by the Department of Employment through the training credits scheme, which is geared to output-related funding. The Department of Employment is not alone in taking the direction of output-related funding, for the DFE is more than hinting at that approach, via its league tables. The pressure on colleges to work to an output-related funding model will become irresistible. Whether it is the right approach is a totally different matter, for one can envisage access opportunities closing to those who are not capable of delivering the appropriate output at the appropriate level, and thus undermining the college's budget. One can also see students not being stretched enough in their studies, because over-stretching might mean failure to deliver the output (i.e., students who have gained awards), and hence the cash. In some shape or form, however, it looks as if output-related funding is here to stay and that implies a system geared to modular delivery for individuals. This reaffirms that the strategy is correct.

The third confirmation lies in the investment in NVQs. Whilst it is not impossible, it is highly unlikely that all the time, money and effort poured into NVQs will be wasted. There is a determination to make them work. The National Education and Training Targets are based on them. Industry-led bodies are committed to them. TECs are geared to them. So NVQs are here to stay, too, and they are modular.

We don't need any more confirmation that the strategy for delivering the curriculum via student-centred learning is correct. That should give us confidence to press ahead.

In managing this quantum leap so that we don't fall flat on our faces, we must next be sure to monitor the implementation of the strategy. Such a fundamental change in approach to curriculum delivery needs careful handling. It would be easy to overlook genuine strains and stresses in the system in the desire to push ahead rapidly. Equally, the comfort of the old delivery methods could be so seductive that we let the initiative slip, defeated by inertia. The monitoring needs to be sensitive, but the implementation process needs to be relentless, because of the clear pattern for the future described above.

Management and staff, therefore, need to be encouraged to know that this move to student-centred learning is not a momentary whim and that there is a determination to see it properly and professionally established. They need to be kept informed of developments, to know what are the agreed implementation targets, what are the rewards for achieving them, what are the penalties for not achieving, and how they are performing against those targets.

The monitoring needs to ensure that staff at all levels have a chance to comment. The programme of change via student-centred learning is too radical for any views to be ignored. Existing communication channels should be programmed to deal with feedback: course team reports, boards of study, academic boards, course evaluations from students, staff and employers – all should be used to ensure success. And the message needs to be clear, that more – whilst meaning different – does not mean worse. There is a natural concern about quality and a natural human resistance to change: these form a powerful alliance. The latter must always be contested; the former needs to be carefully observed. There are assumptions that must be challenged: for example, that that which is in place is bound to be better in quality than that which replaces it. Equally, the reverse must be challenged. In coping with this change, therefore, we must be open to adopting new ideas, impartial in our approach; but in particular, we must be scrupulous in ensuring that the individual student experience is enhanced. In that way, quality will be preserved in the midst of change.

The part played by that which was once a simple library is key to the success of the total strategy. In the same way that further education has now become the centrepiece of the DFE's national strategy, so the area of learning resources is moving centre stage in the college. It must not be allowed to drift into that situation. Careful, strategic planning is required. That will produce a demand for resources which will have to be levered out from the traditional home for those resource, and that will cause pain. As with resources, so with structure. The learning resources area cannot be expected to play its part unless it is given its place in the sun. That, too, may be painful for some. There is no place in the sun, of course, without a return, and learning resources will need to deliver a highly professional service which is derived not from its historic position but from its future aspirations and responsibilities. The college of the future will be looking for leadership as much from its learning resources area as from everywhere else. Directors of learning resources will be among the chief executives of the twenty-first century. Their time – and that of the service areas for which they are responsible – has come.

3

The institutional context: higher education

John Stoddart and Simon Hughes

The context

Society is changing at an unprecedented pace. The decades since the Second World War have been a period of rapid and accelerating technological development, fuelling increased industrial productivity and economic growth. The same technological advance has created a global market-place and intense worldwide competition, within which the operations of manufacturing, services and government have become more knowledge intensive. This rapid pace of change means that knowledge and technical competence very quickly become outdated in technology-driven industries and Europe is faced with growing skills shortages in key areas, such as electronics and information technology, biotechnology and systems engineering. At the same time, demographic shifts mean that fewer young people with recent education will be entering the workforce than in previous years, thus placing greater emphasis on the upgrading and updating of the existing workforce.

These circumstances have served to emphasize the vital relationship between education and training, and industrial competitiveness. Competitive advantage increasingly depends upon having a skilled and competent workforce and the demand for better educated and highly trained people has intensified as a result. The growing awareness of the important role that higher education can play in terms of raising both the quantity and quality of skills relevant to the needs of the economy has, over the past 30 years, become the most significant factor in determining the context within which higher education operates.

During this period, technological change and economic growth have also had a potent and multiplying effect on the expectations and aspirations of successive generations. In the United Kingdom, the spread of car ownership provides one example; despite the fall in average household size, the proportion of households with at least two cars has continued to rise steadily – from only 2 per cent in 1961 to 22 per cent in 1989.[1] Just as economic growth has influenced consumer demand for goods and services, so it has also raised the demand for education, both as a form of consumption and as an investment in the future.

Such economic and social forces have combined to generate a major impact on the education sector within Europe; in fact, over recent years all the European Community member states have experienced growth in the proportion of their population participating in higher education. In a changing and unpredictable world, education must be central to our ambitions for the future development of Europe and its citizens. Higher education will be judged by how well it meets the current and future aspirations for the economy and for society as a whole; it cannot therefore stand apart from the changes taking place all around it. The implications for higher education of these changes are extremely wide ranging and raise questions about virtually all aspects of its role and its contribution to the future development of the economy, society and culture of both Europe and the individual member states.

Expansion and reform

In the United Kingdom, higher education institutions have responded enthusiastically to the new demands made upon them in the past decade: chief amongst these have been: the expansion of student numbers; the widening of access to groups traditionally under-represented in higher education; a growing responsiveness to the needs of both students and employers; and a greater emphasis on quality, efficiency and accountability.

The issues of expansion, access, responsiveness and quality are not new and, within Europe, individual countries have responded to these concerns in different ways for some years. However, a common pattern has emerged in response to these issues in the by-passing of the established universities and the development of an alternative sector of higher education. In many ways, it is the success of these alternative sectors that continues to shape the future development of higher education in Europe.

In the United Kingdom, it has been the former polytechnic and college sector that has played the key role in the expansion of higher education and in meeting new demands for more accessible and responsive institutions. The number of home full-time students in higher education has increased from 217,000 in 1962-3 to over 668,000 in 1990-1[2] and in the 1980s alone the number of students rose by nearly 30 per cent. In addition, there are 287,000 part-time students in higher education, the majority located in the new universities (the former polytechnics) and the colleges. Access to higher education has also been widened. Female students now make up half of all students on full-time first-degree courses, compared to only 41 per cent in 1980, and the number of mature students (aged over 21 years on entry to undergraduate courses, or over 25 for postgraduate) has increased by 77 per cent in the decade to 1990 to stand at over a quarter of a million (excluding those studying at the Open University).

It is the success of the former polytechnics and the colleges in responding to the national need for an expansion of opportunities that has redefined and reshaped higher education in the United Kingdom, and presaged the radical changes contained in the 1992 *Further and Higher Education Act.*[3] The Act extended degree-awarding powers to the polytechnics and other major institutions, granted the polytechnics the right to adopt the title of university and created a framework under which universities, old and new, would in future be able to compete on merit for students and funds. Much progress has been made in recent years and the removal of the binary line is a major step forward. However, a significant challenge remains, namely whether current structures and practices can develop at sufficient pace under the new framework to meet new demands and maintain the quality which has long been a cornerstone of the United Kingdom system.

During the post-war period, the United Kingdom higher education system has changed from being 'a small group of universities and of public institutions, loosely held together, and catering for a minuscule proportion of the population, to a largely centralised system with a sizeable recruitment'.[4] To understand this transformation, it is necessary to consider the reasons for the development of the polytechnic and college sector of higher education and for its subsequent success. Underlying this development has been a fundamental question concerning the purposes of higher education and the type of institutions best suited to addressing those purposes.

The emergence of a new framework

During the past 30 years, the established universities have been widely perceived, rightly or wrongly, as conservative and unresponsive to change. They have represented an autonomous tradition in higher education, which has been somewhat divorced from society at large and from local communities. This tradition of autonomy and conservatism has proved largely inappropriate for meeting the new demands that have been made of higher education – chiefly those of expansion, efficiency and accountability – and has been an important factor in bringing into existence, and sustaining the growth of, an alternative and dynamic sector of higher education outside the universities.

In the United Kingdom, the vehicle for the development of this alternative sector has been the binary policy, whose introduction has often been attributed to Anthony Crosland, the secretary of state between 1965 and 1967. In fact, as Crosland readily acknowledged, a binary or plural system existed long before the 1960s. Alongside the universities in the 1950s there were training colleges under local authority or denominational control, and a strong and growing sector of higher education in further education colleges. The Robbins report of 1963[5] observed that over 40 per cent of students in full-time higher education were studying outside the universities. The contribution of both Robbins and Crosland was to recognize the value of the work being done in the public sector and to conclude that it was entitled to serious consideration in the future development of the nation's higher education system. It was precisely to strengthen this sector that, following the recommendations of the Robbins committee, the Council for National Academic Awards (CNAA) was set up in 1964 to regulate standards and award degrees outside the universities.

Government acceptance of most of the recommendations contained in the Robbins report translated gradual expansion into stated policy and set targets for expansion to 290,000 full-time students by 1967–8. In fact, these targets were exceeded by over 47,000, owing largely to rising numbers in the further education sector and in colleges of education. The White Paper *A Plan for Polytechnics and Other Colleges*[6] set out proposals for a limited number of polytechnics by the amalgamation of colleges of art and design, commerce and technology. The policy was to build up a strong and distinctive sector of higher education which was complementary to the universities and colleges of education. Polytechnics were designed to be comprehensive institutions in the range and character of their work and 'as mixed communities of full-time and part-time teachers and students would as a whole have closer and more direct links with industry, business and the professions'.[7] Furthermore, the government believed that the best results would be achieved by developing higher education along polytechnic lines wherever practicable.

It was thus by a process of evolution that the public sector developed and the new polytechnics were introduced as a development of the major achievements in the local authority provision of higher education. Between 1969 and 1973 a total of 30 polytechnics were formed from amalgamations of well-established colleges with a tradition of teaching vocational subjects. Essentially, the creation of the polytechnics was an attempt by the government to bring higher education closer to the needs of students, employers and the community – under 'social control', as Crosland termed it. In large part, this was a response to the growing demand from prospective students as a result of the 'bulge' (the rise in the post-war birth-rate) and the 'trend' (the increase in the numbers of young people qualified to enter higher education). It also reflected a national concern about the shortage of qualified scientists, engineers, technologists and technicians, which threatened manufacturing industry's long-term ability to compete.

By the early 1970s, despite the difficulties of course recognition and under-funding, the progress of the polytechnics fuelled debate about the purposes of higher education, both liberal and vocational. The debate had previously been focused on traditions and values, but had by now broadened to include the structure of higher education itself, and the declared or perceived missions both of the new institutions and of the sector as a whole. As the polytechnics developed and gained acceptance during the 1970s, coping with rising student numbers continued to be the priority for higher education. However, by 1978-9, expansion was slowing and by the end of the decade actual student numbers were some way below those forecast. In part, this slowing down was due to the economic crisis of the mid-1970s and a fall in the age participation rate. Nevertheless, by 1979 the polytechnics had widened their scope, established themselves as serving both national and local needs and had met excess student demand – in part because of the 'pooling' arrangements which left them relatively free of central control over recruitment. The assimilation (except in Scotland) of the colleges of education into the public sector of higher education in the mid-1970s significantly strengthened the polytechnics, as undoubtedly the transfer of the former colleges helped to build up their provision in the humanities and social sciences.

During the 20-year period of steady expansion from 1960, a broad consensus held in higher education that maintained a somewhat uneasy balance between the needs of the economy and the preservation of academic freedom and autonomy. However, higher education was to be confronted with a 'fundamental question', namely 'the extent to which consensual arrangements and assumptions that generally worked well during the long post-war period of its expansion can cope with the much more stringent conditions likely to prevail in the 1980s and 1990s'.[8]

The early 1980s marked a significant change in the development of higher education in the United Kingdom. This was the beginning of the end for the autonomous and elitist tradition of higher education and the start of its replacement by a new, more open and accessible system based in the service tradition and emphasizing flexibility, responsiveness, efficiency and accountability. The expansion of higher education and its consequent impact on public expenditure had given the state a greater interest in its effectiveness, efficiency and accountability. As a result, a significant shift towards stronger central control took place, which was intended to enable the expansion of the system at the least cost.

Initially little more than part of a package of moves to limit public expenditure, a policy evolved which can be seen clearly in the White Paper *Higher education: meeting the challenge*.[9] Expansion was required. The need for quality and efficiency was held to justify more selectively funded research 'targeted with attention to prospects for commercial exploitation'. Funding was to be put on a contractual basis through the funding councils and performance against those contracts was to be monitored. Higher education was encouraged to respond more closely to the needs of the market, and institutions that worked more closely with business and industry would be rewarded. Since 1987 this policy has provided a momentum for change, the impact of which has been felt throughout the system. The driving force behind it has been perceived economic need and a continuing drive to gain competitive advantage for the United Kingdom economy.

This policy was pursued in two ways. First, higher education was to work within a 'market-led and multi-funded setting'[10] and to respond to the needs of the market. Secondly, there was a shift towards greater central authority in higher education in which 'academic norms and modes of self-governance had given way to powerful objective-setting by the central authorities'.[11] This central thrust set the context for the changes in the latter 1980s and 1990s which saw first the incorporation of the polytechnics and subsequently the creation of a single university sector, albeit a very diverse one.

The institutional response

How have institutions responded to rapid environmental change and, in particular, the sometimes conflicting demands for expansion, access, responsiveness, cost effectiveness, accountability and quality?

A major and significant difference should be noted between the former polytechnics in the United Kingdom and the non-university institutions elsewhere in Europe, in that the former polytechnics have not been restrained in either their growth aspirations or their profile. From the start it has been accepted that the polytechnics could teach at undergraduate, masters and doctoral level (offering CNAA awards) and could offer subjects in the arts, humanities and business and management, as well as in science and technology. The *Fachhochschulen* in Germany, in contrast, are more specialized, providing studies with a practical bias – mainly in engineering, business administration, social science, design and agriculture. It has also been recognized that the polytechnics provided courses of equivalent status to universities and had a mission to meet excess student demand and not only to respond to the needs of business and industry. This breadth and mix has been a central factor in their success.

The achievements of the former polytechnics and the colleges have in many ways been remarkable. In the decade 1979–89, enrolment on full-time courses expanded by some 50 per cent in the polytechnics and colleges, as against only 12 per cent in the universities, whilst at the same time expenditure for a fte student in the public sector fell by some 25 per cent in real terms. By the end of the 1980s, over 50 per cent of the students studying on higher education courses in the United Kingdom were doing so in polytechnics and colleges.

That expansion was steered nationally, but planned and managed locally. Until 1989 and the incorporation of the polytechnics under the Education Reform Act,[12] polytechnics worked within a tight framework. The plethora of controlling and monitoring bodies to which the polytechnics were accountable – LEAs, the CNAA, HMI, the National Advisory Board for Public Sector Higher Education (NAB), regional advisory councils – whilst irksome and frustrating at times, has produced institutions with purpose, commitment and a tradition of accountability. They are used to planning, monitoring and responding to new demands and have developed an approach which is entrepreneurial and innovative and which believes firmly in educational opportunity.

The former polytechnics' record in managing growth and change is a remarkable achievement. It is also linked to significant educational developments. Arguably most, if not all, of the major educational innovations of recent years in the United Kingdom have occurred in the polytechnic and college sector. These include: the pioneering of new courses to meet emerging occupational needs; the establishment of access programmes and outreach; the development of integrated work experience in partnership with employers; opportunities for students to study a mix of subjects of their own choice, to a level and at a pace determined by themselves, according to their circumstances; the development of CATS possibilities and of bridges and ladders between qualifications and between institutions; and the rapid expansion of part-time higher education opportunities and of continuing professional development. All these are now part of mainstream higher education activity and are shaping the future development of the whole system.

Traditionally the former polytechnics and the colleges have shown a willingness to innovate and an enthusiasm for responding rapidly and flexibly to local, regional and national needs, both educational and vocational. It is worth noting that the rate of development of business and management education since the 1960s has been greater than for any other type of vocational education. It was within the polytechnic and college sector that this expansion was most marked and as such it provides a significant example of the responsiveness of these institutions to the expressed needs of individuals and the economy. From only 15 CNAA first-degree courses in business studies in 1969, the number rose to 41 by 1978. By 1990–1 there were over 42,000 students following CNAA approved courses in business and management in response to national demand.

In considering such achievements it is important to acknowledge the contribution of the CNAA, which was wound up following the granting of degree-awarding powers to the new universities under the 1992 Act.[13] By operating in increasing partnership with institutions, the CNAA has laid important foundations for the future success of the single university sector.

A number of issues are worth noting. Importantly, the statutes of the CNAA required that the awards it made were comparable in standard with awards granted for higher education in the United Kingdom, including the universities. The need over many years to meet high CNAA standards of quality control and assurance has created a shared commitment to the importance of quality and has enabled considerable experience to be gained in the operation of systematic quality control procedures. In part, this occurred through the establishment of a national network for peer review which gave confidence to institutions, students, employers and government that standards were being maintained and enhanced. This provided a firm basis for expansion and innovation and supported institutions in increasing access and developing flexible approaches such as modular courses, credit transfer and credit accumulation. The CNAA also played an important role in gaining the general acceptance that courses in higher education should have as a principal aim the development of the high level and subject-free skills and attitudes valued by employers.

Funding

These achievements have to be set in the context of the growing demands placed upon higher education and a squeeze on funding characterized by a shrinking unit of resource. Since 1988, there has been a 20 per cent decline in the unit of resource across all higher education institutions as numbers have risen sharply and national funding policies have forced down the relative cost.[14] The accusation of under-funding in higher education has been made throughout the 1980s and a strong argument for a more realistic financing strategy has been put forward by the Council for Industry and Higher Education.[15] Adequate investment in buildings and equipment is clearly significant if higher education is to fulfil its mission, whilst maintaining and enhancing the quality of teaching and research. However, this must be matched by new definitions of the purpose and practice of higher education and by institutional management that is responsive, efficient and accountable.

The pattern throughout the 1980s of greater central direction in higher education was perhaps first seen in the establishment of the (NAB), which was to provide a national framework for planning.

The later transformation of the NAB into the Polytechnics and Colleges Funding Council (PCFC) removed the last vestiges of local authority control over planning and replaced it with a much stronger central authority.

Under the PCFC, greater central control was pursued through an increase in tuition fees and corresponding reduction in the block grant made to institutions, together with the introduction of a system of contracting designed to lead to 'greater precision in the specification of what is expected of institutions in return for public funding.'[16] It was further reinforced by requirements that institutions submit strategic plans for funding council approval. Elsewhere, institutions were also encouraged to develop closer links with business and industry and here too they were subject to central controls. For instance, funds obtained through the Department of Employment's Enterprise in Higher Education Initiative were subject to audit to ensure objectives were achieved.

The rise of managerialism

The polytechnics were established to be responsive, cost-effective institutions with a high degree of accountability. Higher education has to be viewed in the context of the economy and society; in a rapidly changing world it cannot stand still. The first point to be made, therefore, is that to cope with change, institutions must identify the key changes and seek to adapt to the environment in which they operate. Undoubtedly, the environment is a very complex one and there are risks, but the difficulties of predicting, forecasting and responding to a changing environment cannot be used as an excuse. In the past, it might be suggested that most in higher education have sat back until change has been forced upon them rather than attempting to look ahead, foresee changes and adapt. Beyond this, higher education must also seek to influence the environment in an active way rather than to respond after the event as in crisis management.

In both the new and the older universities there is now undoubtedly a greater emphasis on management skills in the running of institutions. The requirement to produce strategic plans for funding councils, the greater freedom in recruitment of student numbers, the development of performance indicators, increased accountability for the use of public funds and increasing competition between institutions for both students and funds inevitably require management and leadership.

The 1980s have witnessed a decline in the committee system of administration and its partial replacement by line management structures, as institutions have attempted to improve efficiency and respond more rapidly to the external environment. This can be seen in the reduced role for university senates, as a result of the crisis in the early 1980s and the recommendations of the Jarrett report,[17] and for academic boards following incorporation which has given greater prominence to the role of the chief executive. As a consequence of the dual traditions of both hierarchy and consensus, academic institutions contain systems based on both executive and committee structures.[18] The need to respond to external challenges and to implement priorities has led to the rise of managerialism in higher education institutions, which can be seen in the new universities in the dual roles of vice-chancellor and chief executive.

Challenges and opportunities

The rapid and radical reshaping of higher education that has taken place following the *Further and Higher Education Act*[19] has seen the establishment of a single university sector of higher education consisting of some 80 universities, which by the year 2000 will be catering for over one million undergraduate students. This will inevitably mean wide diversification between types of institution and indeed within institutions; between those concentrating mainly on undergraduate teaching, those emphasizing professional and postgraduate education with selective strength in near-market research, and those with strong international centres of excellence in research. The strength of the sector is its diversity and individual institutions must position themselves according to their particular strengths.

The change of title from polytechnic to university does not mean any change of mission for the new universities; rather it would be more accurate to say that the reform of the system has sought to bring the old universities into the service tradition. The new universities will continue as student-driven institutions committed to vocational and professional education; to meeting the needs of business and industry for highly skilled employees; to operating on a local, national and increasingly international basis; and to widening participation in higher education. Many of the old universities are likely to move towards this model as institutions seek to place themselves within the new sector.

Nor is it likely that these changes will simply result in the creation of a new binary line to divide further education and higher education. Higher education no longer operates in isolation from society and vocational education has particular significance, standing as it does at the interface of two rapidly changing worlds, those of compulsory schooling and of employment. In the move towards developing a learning society, there needs to be a smooth path between all sectors. The development of associate college schemes, franchise and access arrangements, compacts and accreditation of prior learning suggests that this process is well underway. Changes to the school curriculum, new targets for the expansion of further education and the development of a framework for vocational qualifications will all have implications for higher education in terms of the volume and nature of its customers. Only a close partnership between all involved in education and training will ensure its success.

With modest economic growth forecast to the end of the century, the central challenge for higher education continues to be the question of how future expansion is to be achieved in the context of a falling unit of resource, whilst maintaining and enhancing quality. Student numbers have expanded rapidly in response to increasing demand, so rapidly in fact that the government has taken steps to encourage consolidation over the next three years of the mid-1990s and to redirect student demand towards science and engineering, so that targets are reached through controlled expansion. However, the real demand for higher education will almost certainly continue to grow, placing even greater emphasis on institutional management and leadership, and raising a large number of questions about the structure and content of courses and qualifications. Managing this growth will have to be achieved within a framework that encourages both competition and collaboration between institutions and within an increasingly European and international context.

Institutions are actively addressing this challenge by giving consideration to new structures and curriculum developments that will enhance the learning experience and prepare students for lifelong learning. The reorganization of the academic year, the development of new strategies for teaching and learning, the development of a national credit framework and increasing opportunities for students to study at their own pace are encouraging steps forward. The changing nature of the student experience and the difficulties associated with student finance also present a significant challenge to all involved in higher education. In the words of the current secretary of state, 'a lot of change is behind us, more is still to come'.[20]

References

1 Central Statistical Office, *Social trends* 22, HMSO, 1992.
2 Department for Education, *Education statistics for the UK (Table 26)*, HMSO, 1992.
3 *Further and Higher Education Act, 1992*, HMSO, 1992.
4 Becher, T. and Kogan, M., *Process and structure in higher education*, Routledge, 1992.
5 *Higher education; report of the Committee on Higher Education*, Cmnd 2154, HMSO, 1963. (The Robbins Report)
6 Department of Education and Science, *A plan for polytechnics and other colleges*, Cmnd 3006, HMSO, 1966.
7 *Ibid.*
8 Williams, G., 'Survival in a harsh climate', D. Jaques and J. Richardson (eds.), *The future of higher education*, SRHE and NFER–Nelson, 1985.
9 Department of Education and Science, *Higher education: meeting the challenge*, Cm 114, HMSO, 1987.
10 Baker, K.,'Higher education: the next 25 years', speech delivered at Lancaster University, 1989.
11 Becher and Kogan, *op. cit.*
12 *Education Reform Act*, HMSO, 1988.
13 *Further and Higher Education Act, op. cit.*
14 Robertson, D., 'Courses, qualifications and the empowerment of learners', *Higher education: expansion and reform*, IPPR, London, 1992.
15 Council for Industry and Higher Education, *Investing in diversity*, CIHE, 1992.
16 Department of Education and Science, *Higher education: meeting the challenge, op. cit.*
17 Committee of Vice-Chancellors and Principals, *Report of the Steering Committee for Efficiency Studies in Universities*, CVCP and HMSO, 1985. (The Jarrett report)
18 Becher and Kogan, *op. cit.*
19 *Further and Higher Education Act, op. cit.*
20 Patten, J., Speech delivered at the inauguration of the University of Portsmouth, 1992.

4

Organizing resources for learning

Allen Armsby

This chapter examines how college libraries have evolved from a traditional print base into multi-media resource centres. It is not a fully detailed account, but offers the impressions and philosophy of one who was involved in the transition and who created several resource centres. The chapter also discusses the total learning resources concept for whole college development and some of the ideas behind convergence.

At any conference, course or meeting aimed at college resources managers, there will be a wider spread of job titles now than in the past. Librarians, heads of library services, learning resources managers, directors of learning resources and many other titles will be represented. There is nothing new in variation of titles, but the span of responsibilities they imply is probably greater now than previously. The 'college librarian' is not yet an endangered species, but numbers are declining! Some people have responsibility for all college learning resources, others for miscellaneous parts of a service forged largely by college politics rather than by any educational rationale. Some may have no responsibilities beyond the library service, but the scope of that library service will be larger than that term encompassed in the past.

One of the most significant changes in college libraries has been the greater range of print and audiovisual resources available. A visitor to such a library today would be surprised if it did not offer audiovisual and/or computing resources. In the recent past, their inclusion would have occasioned surprise – even, in some cases, doubt as to whether it was appropriate to include them within such an environment; such has been the extent of recent change. During the past 30 years the broadening of librarians' responsibilities can count as one of the major successes of the library profession and the colleges. Fears that new media would push the book into oblivion have proved ill-founded; the wide variety of media is seen now to be more complementary to traditional stock than was expected. The ability of librarians to adapt to changing opportunities and find new roles within their institutions has been remarkable. This chapter is an acknowledgment of their flexibility and interest in providing a knowledge and information base relevant to students and lecturing staff. In recent years, some librarians have been catapulted into accepting greater responsibilities in an almost unseemly rush generated by curriculum change and financial and organizational upheavals within their colleges.

Today's easy acceptance of the need to provide audiovisual resources in libraries has not always been seen to be natural. Thirty years ago, such ideas were regarded by some as anarchic and controversial. With the enormous benefit of hindsight, some of that debate now seems rather absurd, but it was the stuff of which meetings, conferences and articles were made. Those times in the evolution of college libraries were a period of great enthusiasms and of exploring new activities, possibilities and responsibilities.

I began by remarking upon the wide variety of titles to be found amongst college librarians. I shall refer throughout to the librarian, on the understanding that the title encompasses all the titles in so far as the evolution of resources centres is concerned; but I recognize that, in the latter part of the chapter, the term may not be synonymous with someone running a total learning resources service.

The development of resources centres has not been the same in any two colleges. The ancestry of the different development routes was identified in a thesis by T. A. Whitworth in 1969.[1] This was, for librarians, a hugely significant piece of research, written by one who was not a librarian but a scientist. The idea of role identification was then a comparatively new sociological concept. To apply it within the constrained field of college librarianship was a stroke of genius. Librarianship as a profession had not been a major primary focus for research. The research was timely and supportive of librarians, making practical suggestions for the development of their professional role. What made the research so interesting was that, in the newly developing colleges of the 1960s, librarians were seeking to identify what their role was. Technology was felt to be the spirit of the age and the key to the future. Many colleges had a strong technical bias and it was felt that, somehow, the library ought to reflect that. But how?

Many college librarians felt that their relationship to the teaching process should be closer and that the library needed to go beyond providing books. Many college libraries offered little more than a quiet refuge for the chosen few. Craft students were either banned, or allowed into the library as a 'treat' (though whether *their* view of this was sought may be doubted!). The management of such environments could hardly be regarded as challenging. In essence, college management required the library to do little more than be there, open and close. This may seem an unfair judgement but, unlike today's situation, students spent most or all of their time in classrooms or workshops. Very few were full-time; most were part-time, apprentices whose time in the college was closely regulated by their employers. Students visited the library on their own, or as part of liberal studies, or not at all. The gradual growth of full-time courses is an important factor to consider when charting the rise of more sophisticated library services. Today, when links between curriculum and library use are better understood, it may seem surprising that some students ever entered those early libraries. That many did was greatly to their credit.

> Undue stress on the part of the Principal on the use of conventional teaching methods associated with the classroom and laboratory is the death knell to the establishment of the library as the hub of the educational community. Too often one finds the library a showpiece, demonstrating the traditional atmosphere of learning, but this will be the glamour of the cover girl rather than the beauty of motherhood.

Thus wrote Wright in 1968.[2] Set against the rather limited view of the role of a college library at that time, it is not surprising that the concept of an active, busy, student-centred environment did not match the views of those who knew exactly what a library was for!

Whitworth turned the tables on librarians by daring to classify them. He designated six main categories: non-tutorial, non-educationalists; non-tutorial educationalists; tutorial non-educationalists; tutorial educationists; teacher-librarians; semi-tutorial librarians and others. The views of librarians varied from those who believed that interaction between libraries, teaching and learning was complex to those who believed the opposite. Here, with the identification for the first time of such differing views on their roles within colleges, we can begin to understand why we have in colleges in the 1990s, librarians holding such diverse functions. Each of the different types of librarians identified by Whitworth had its own attitudes towards the relative importance of learning resources. A measure of how much has altered over the past 30 years is that there are surely no librarians in colleges now who do not believe that libraries are central to the educational process, that all media have a part to play in supporting the information needs of staff and students, and that the responsibility of the library is to spread its understanding of access, organization and flexibility into other areas of service within the college.

Within Whitworth's thesis was a section on the supervision of a 'learning resources centre'. He asked: 'Are you (or members of the library staff) responsible for the storage or supervision of audiovisual aids for the use of the college as a whole?' The answers to this question were: Yes – 60 (20%); No – 203 (67%); Partially – 38 (13%).

He then asked if the supervision of a learning resources centre was a function of the library. The answers were:

	Essential or important	Not part of the librarian's work	Minor importance or no opinion
Librarians	132 (48%)	40 (14%)	106 (38%)
Staff	50 (26%)	90 (48%)	48 (26%)
Senior staff	16 (20%)	42 (51%)	24 (29%)
Other staff	34 (32%)	48 (45%)	24 (23%)
Students	69 (35%)	70 (35%)	61 (30%)

Note that librarians were divided amongst themselves on the importance of the learning resources concept. Staff and students were less than impressed. It would have been more worrying had the results been the other way around. After all, one should expect professionals to lead, if only weakly as in this instance. Not surprisingly, of the librarians in favour of the resources centre concept it was the 'tutorial educationalists' and the 'non-tutorial educationalists' who led the way – in other words, the two types who identified their roles most closely with the educational and curriculum role of the library.

One of Whitworth's objectives was to study how librarians viewed themselves and their libraries. Many librarians felt marginal to their institutions and lacking in status. Whitworth made two important points. Firstly, if librarians wished to move centre stage they had to redefine their role by becoming closer to the educational process. Second, adopting the concepts underlying resource centres would increase their power.

There are strong reasons for advocating that the library should hold a central position in the educational work of a technical college. Since the learning tradition in the colleges is not library based, librarians have to act in a positive manner to achieve centrality. While informal methods of persuasion of staff and students are extremely valuable (and possibly essential), there are some disadvantages to a complete reliance on this approach. A more permanent measure of centrality may be achieved by increasing the formal power of the librarian within the college structure. Three possible methods of achieving this aim are by undertaking tutorial activities with students, by developing educational advisory activities with staff and by supervising a 'learning resources centre' containing audio and visual aids for the use of the college as a whole.

This last point went to the heart of the matter and sent a clear message to college librarians. Most did not have teaching qualifications, but they did have the ability to organize more than books. They felt able to offer their colleges a broader vision of what a library could be, given support, and they had sufficient management skills to run more than a unitary service, provided that they were given control of a greater part of the college's resources. The concept of a learning resources centre seemed to answer all these needs. Not everyone agreed; some librarians felt that involvement with media other than books would diversify and weaken their role by making them vulnerable to the charge of empire building. This school claimed that it was better to remain within the limited, traditional political and professional power base of the library.

It was also difficult to argue against one very real problem – funding. For many librarians, funding was minuscule and the move out of books into other media hard to justify. Other librarians felt, however, that to widen the resources base would in time strengthen not only their own position but, ultimately, the book collection as well. Whitworth had raised the spectre of power, the desire for which few are prepared to acknowledge, by pointing out that to remain sheltered within a traditional library was not the most effective way of playing a greater role within the college. The fact that so many librarians felt that they were uninvolved and insignificant in the eyes of senior management, but at the same time were not inclined to move into new areas of influence, seems almost beyond comprehension today – until we reflect upon the magnitude of the change offered, as set against the professional norms of the time. This redefining of roles and the interplay of political power and professional service is still with us today. Even within the universities, power struggles are in evidence as librarians move into the territory of other services, including computing, media services, student services and reprographics.

One of the suggestions Whitworth made was that librarians should play a more central role in the educational process. At that time, a new type of librarian was being created – the tutor-librarian. One cannot do justice to this topic here; suffice it to say that the concept had no single standard set of duties – each college had its own ideas. Some tutor-librarian posts represented both the librarian's post and a tutorial function, which varied from a full teaching commitment to a more reasonable 50 per cent teaching allocation. Some tutor-librarians were appointed in a supporting role to the librarian and organized readers' awareness sessions and liberal studies lectures. Some had no formal class contact but were appointed to talk to groups as requested by lecturing staff. More significantly, some were required to organize their libraries in accordance with the educational objectives of the college and to support new teaching methods. This meant that instead of becoming a slave to teaching, an element of experiment was involved. Those tutor-librarians fortunate enough to have such a remit found that moving towards the resource centre concept was rather easier for them than for other librarians. Tutor-librarians were in academic posts, while most other college librarians were on administrative conditions. There was a third, hybrid group of librarians who had administrative (NJC) conditions and academic (Burnham) salaries. This was a neat managerial solution where a small staff of librarians was required to be on duty in the college out of term time. It is perhaps a pity that union squabbles and professional envy affected and continue to affect this arrangement.

Coincidentally with the appearance of tutor-librarians, there appeared upon the scene another set of key players. The new breed were called media technologists, resource lecturers or educational technologists. In some colleges, the librarian actually fitted that role, merging interest in librarianship with the media. Other librarians were content to allow some other individual to work with technologies with which they personally had little sympathy. There were mergers or truces as the educational technologist ran the hardware and the librarians looked after the software. There was also the final option of the two empires ignoring each other and going down parallel paths. In some cases, because educational technologists may have been – unlike librarians – trained teachers, they found it easier to slip into the academic role and to be included on course teams, academic boards and so on, marginalizing some of the librarians. For educational technologists, the concept that librarians could organize audiovisual software or look after audiovisual equipment, or integrate the two into a single service, roused intense debate and scepticism. Some were absorbed in the blossoming technology, rather than the educational implications of using it. The concept that students should use the machines without a lecturer's guidance was considered dangerous. However, jointly between librarians, tutor-librarians and educational technologists, there was an increasing use of audiovisual software and equipment in colleges. Possibly because so many of the education colleges contained staff who taught technology, there were individual lecturing staff willing to use new technology in their teaching and to support new services. Technology was the spirit of the age, something one wanted to be caught up in, even if it led into areas of doubt and error.

Librarians were involved in many decisions and arguments with regard to the setting up of resources centres. The pro camp held the high moral ground. Their arguments included the need for the library to encompass the whole of human knowledge and experience; the importance of acknowledging that books were not supreme in their dominance of the knowledge market; and that different experiences and stimulations made a book on Beethoven as valid as listening to his music. Lecturers were beginning, even within the structured organization of the teaching day, to encourage project work and group explorations. There was the beginning of a change of attitude, towards encouraging lecturers to undertake teacher training, and these courses encouraged staff to look at new media. They could be used more easily than some of the old technologies and it was these staff who began to require colleges to establish audiovisual workshops and resource committees to foster developments. In addition, librarians put audiovisual resources into their libraries to encourage students into the library. It seemed likely that to provide records, cassettes and films would change students' attitudes to the library for the better. Later, the provision of microcomputers in libraries served a similar function.

Speaking against these arguments were the massed voices of practical doom. Firstly, it was said that these technologies were meant for classroom use and not for individual students. The range of available resources was limited and lacked any real mass appeal compared with books, so purchasing such resources would not advance the knowledge base of the library in any meaningful way. The equipment needed was beyond the reach of the average library and had no real place amongst the books. Equipment had the potential to create disturbing noises and what would happen if it broke down? Librarians were not trained to handle it. All the resources (unlike the books!) would be stolen or damaged. Above all, the small staff resources of the libraries were a major barrier, stopping any initiative whatsoever; new responsibilities were out of the question. The real problem was finance. For librarians having to make do on small budgets and with an inadequate basic stock, the thought of taking on new formats was too much to contemplate. These financial constraints are still with us today. How many further education establishments can afford to purchase the many excellent commercial training videos? Video discs are sometimes purchased as specimens to show to students studying IT. Perhaps in this era of the mass lecture, the economics of purchasing these expensive items may be turned on its head and resources begin to flow into creating larger collections of items and sharing them cost-effectively between greater numbers of students.

Those college librarians who wished to follow the resources route had some successful role models to look towards for ideas, enthusiasm and experience. The first of these influences was the colleges of education. Many had extensive teaching practice collections containing slides, posters, filmstrips, filmloops, pictures, games, models, even stuffed birds. The librarians in these colleges found the challenge of widening the definition of libraries satisfying and adopted innovative ways of maintaining and recording collections, ensuring that new media were not refused a home simply because of administrative difficulties. Although the purpose of these collections was different from those of the library of a further education college, the easy acceptance by the colleges of education of the educational and curriculum worth of the material was an important influence; there was no reason why college of further education lecturers would not be grateful for similar collections of curriculum support material in their colleges.

Schools were another major influence. The Schools Council project on resource-based learning helped many college librarians. The curriculum and teaching methods were changing rapidly in schools; many teachers wanted the educational experience of children to be less passive. Children were allowed to explore topics for themselves; they could move around, use equipment, work in groups. The use of material was cross-disciplinary; many schools created mini-resource centres, even organizing the entire school around them. These centres had a diversity of material, making use of everything that could be brought to hand. Money for books was just as scarce then as now, but many schools used low-tech resources, such as newspapers, magazines, posters and illustrations, as the basis of their collections. There are parallels with present-day college libraries, which have built up collections of support material using newspapers, magazines, handouts, transparencies, annual reports and so on to supply the needs of students. In the early days of general studies, the study of current affairs was in vogue: race relations, population, transport, energy, law and order, drugs were much in demand and even a low-tech resource base was enough to encourage greater use of the library. Today's libraries have similar demands for information within General Certificate of Secondary Education (GCSE), A-levels, business studies courses and more – all requiring access to CD-ROM, Prestel, Campus 2000 and online information services. But these high-tech solutions have not eradicated the need for the same types of information service.

In some cases, to create resource centres, schools literally pulled out everything they had from their cupboards. Many college resource centres were begun in similar ways, with teaching staff donating material to be held centrally for everyone to use. One way of assisting resource centres in colleges was to match donations with new money to encourage more donations. Also in schools, teaching staff were released to create resources for the common good; this is happening again in colleges, 30 years later, with staff being released to create learning packages for a whole college in curriculum workshops.

A fascinating result of the rise of these collections was the approach taken by some schools, often without librarians, to tackle the classification and information retrieval problems posed by these eclectic collections. Material of different physical forms had to be brought together at a recording stage so that it could be found subsequently by the student from a subject standpoint. The fact that material on dinosaurs might exist in a book, as a poster, a set of slides and so on, meant that systems which coordinated these various media had to be devised. The schools were adventurous and their explorations of cataloguing, subject indexing, punched cards, broad topic banding and record keeping were in advance of practice in most colleges. It is important to recognize the role that the Schools Councils took in these initiatives and to acknowledge the practical and inspirational role of the Inner London Education Authority (ILEA), which created an exciting resource centre in Kennington and encouraged their school librarians to be adventurous and involved with their teachers.

Soon, school resource centres were being used to create, as well as store, resources. Advances in photocopiers, transparency makers, cameras, video cameras and the like meant that one could make resources oneself – a very different experience from the traditional librarian waiting for the next book to be published! The new machines and materials allowed librarians to explore technical, production and creative solutions and helped to eliminate the feeling of being a passive provider. One could become more closely involved with the students as a problem solver. The concept of service widened and many considerations about what a librarian 'should' do became irrelevant. The role became 'whatever the librarian wanted it to be'. By exploring new ground, librarians gained practical experience and could help and encourage teaching staff, who were anxious to become involved but lacked technical know-how. Making resources to fit the needs of a lecturer was rewarding and changed the formerly separate roles into complementary professions with common objectives. Resources could be created to fit exactly with teaching, fill gaps with items not commercially available, and build up material for students who were now being directed to use the library on an individual basis for longer periods.

This same level of creative excitement is with us in the 1990s, as desk-top publishing allows librarians to make their own library and user guides, bibliographies, study guides, forms, notices and the like. The freedom to design, manipulate and produce publications in-house has resulted in much new student support material. The ease of production generates opportunities for collection exploitation, with all the advantages of speedy production and in-house control.

A great debate revolved around the problem of integrating software into library stock. All the media – filmstrips, slides, games, records, tapes and cassettes – had a different physical format; this presented a substantial practical problem. It was argued that format was irrelevant, that material should be placed on the shelves, with different media on the same topics filed together. Underlying this approach was the belief that audiovisual resources were just another information source and that therefore they should not be distinguished in any way. The logic of this was unassailable, but physical problems prevented many librarians from following that route. Shelves of books intermingled with cassettes, boxed kits and records presented not only a challenge to library assistants to keep shelves tidy, but exposed material to the risk of being removed as it was impossible to protect items individually. The security issue was real. Resource centres were frequently given material by teaching staff, for use by the students, but were expected to have it available for lecturers to use in their teaching cycle. To lose material was to break faith and could lead to material being withdrawn back to staff offices. One solution was to integrate the packaging but to keep the actual software at a counter, as record shops do today. This was sensible but expensive (in staff time) to administer.

Another method was to store audiovisual software in specialized facilities but to provide integrated access to all material via the catalogue. This facilitated use, and ensured security. It meant that material would be found by subject enquirers, but did not cater for the browser. Other libraries built separate audiovisual areas with software on open access and the hardware close to hand. Audiovisual librarians began to appear, charged with building collections, recording whatever material existed in the college and exploiting the stock for students and staff. Librarians were becoming available who were willing and able to take on these audiovisual positions, so there was now both somewhere to place new technology and staff to exploit the collections.

It might be a dangerous generalization, but the chances are that when microcomputers first appeared, libraries with such specialized areas found it easier to exploit them. From the first, these computers aroused huge interest. To help students use them, it was vital to have staff skilled in their use. Once a cassette, record or set of slides is located, the students can be left to themselves; computers are a more immediate attention-seeker and the student needs help if a proper service is to be given.

A new curriculum initiative that had a particular effect upon resource centres was open and flexible learning – a concept upon which libraries were built in the first place. The Manpower Services Commission (MSC) and the Open Tech offered opportunity and funding for librarians to move into the resources centre concept. College libraries were the perfect place to test out the experimental learning material that was being produced. They could offer support to individual students and access to equipment over a long period of time, and had the organization to back up the resources. Many libraries were able to take advantage, though in some cases political attitudes hampered results. Other stimuli to thinking came from the National Extension College, National Council for Educational Technology (NCET), Open University, Further Education Unit (FEU), Open College and others. Many college libraries were willing to adapt and change to fit new requirements. In other colleges, these initiatives were pursued with vigour but regarded exclusively as an academic, departmental concern, not a central resource issue. New resources areas, open learning facilities and the like were sometimes set up independently of the library, and not infrequently independently of each other! In other colleges, they were joined together physically, but managed as separate services. They were often managed by teaching staff, who then set about creating 'libraries' of open learning material – something a professional librarian could have accomplished more economically, and with better collection management. Some of these new areas were staffed by smaller teams or even a single member of lecturing staff. As jobs became centred around selling the concept of open learning, so the 'open learning centre' itself became characterized by being more often closed than open! For this reason and no other, librarians were often able to take them over and organize them professionally.

The debate about the ability of librarians to go beyond the operational management of open learning areas reflected strangely the earlier debate over the role of tutor-librarians. Are librarians capable of running and organizing academic services, or should that be left solely to academics? Can librarians offer counselling and study support to individual students? Have librarians a role in the accreditation process? These are all questions that individual colleges responded to in their own way. For some college librarians, the concept of becoming involved with open learning seemed a natural extension of their role, although it cannot be said that these individual cases constitute a *prima-facie* case entitling all librarians to do it. It is possible to pick out the opposing arguments in this debate. Either departments accept that open learning is a natural part of their work and develop their courses accordingly, training lecturing staff to cope with the needs of the students; or, if departments do not wish to undertake open learning as a departmental initiative, they should be content to know that it exists elsewhere in the college, with librarians handling the work. If the lecturing staff were not willing to handle the challenge of open learning, then there was no reason why librarians should not be active in this field. A library or resource centre can form a sound base for the more flexible mode of delivery, and professional librarians are able to support the needs of the learners by providing them with practical skills, encouragement and resources.

Another major stimulus for change was the Business and Technology Education Council (BTEC). They were interested in the resources available to students, both on their courses and centrally. They asked for information about resources to be included in the submissions that colleges made for new or revalidated courses. Resource provision was high on the list of priorities for moderators, who checked the actual resource base against the submission during moderating visits. If a librarian was involved in creating the submission or participating in moderation visits, s/he could study resource provision with the course team, prior to new courses coming into the college – pre-planning! BTEC were rarely able to insist on certain resources being provided before courses were put in place, but lack of suitable provision was normally noted by the moderator and reported to the college principal.

BTEC also raised the profile of information and study skills, which now have widespread acceptance and are integrated into many courses. The accent on such skills raised questions about the facilities available to support numeracy, literacy, language and allied skills. Colleges began to create curriculum workshops to help students with remedial materials, tutorials or access to equipment. Typically, the stock of these workshops is specialized, with a high percentage of resources developed in-house. Usually, lecturing staff with the required subject expertise ran them, but it soon became obvious that to teach in them and organize them at the same time was difficult, and could be carried out more efficiently by library staff. Frequently, the workshops were run in partnership between lecturing staff, undertaking tutorials and one-to-one guidance; and librarians, responsible for the organization of the workshops. These workshops are of proven benefit to students and are currently on the increase in colleges.

The setting up of these workshops led to some confusion, with college managers, departmental heads, librarians and lecturing staff all having different views on their function. Were the students in class contact or free time? Could any department send students to use the workshops? If so, whose students were they? Whose job was it to teach them? Which department paid the bill? Which department was accorded the all-important (because resource-generating) ftes? Were the workshops for full-time or part-time students? Could they be used by classes or individuals? Should they contain educational technology, videos and the like? Was this not the province of open learning? Despite this, there are excellent examples of workshops within colleges, and the concept is able to deal with present accreditation and modularization processes. A further effect of workshops has been the development of learning material production units, using desk-top publishing and enhanced reprographics facilities. This is especially helpful for remedial or back-up material.

A far-reaching BTEC decision was to make information usage a core skill. The result has been to make more computers available for students in all subject areas. Workshops are satisfactory environments for students dealing with information technology to retrieve information, and for those trying to type up notes, word-process an essay or complete a spreadsheet.

The end result of all these changes is that college librarians now have a wide variety of functions. There is no single model for success. Individual perceptions of their role have influenced librarians to some extent, but so have the attitude of senior managers, colleges' ability to adapt to new initiatives, power vacuums and the librarian's ability to take fleeting opportunities. Librarians are now responsible for curriculum workshops, media services, reprographics, student services, open learning, information technology and television studios, as well as libraries. This variety is tribute to the versatility and flexibility of librarians. Brewer[3] has begun to make sense out of these differing structures and to piece them together in terms of their educational and learning support strategies.

The lack of a single framework describing the role of learning resources has bedevilled librarians for many years. In recent years, libraries and other college services have been more closely monitored by management. Senior managers have been given responsibility for learning resources, but this has not necessarily resulted in clear frameworks or principles being created. Opportunities to remove old divisions have not been taken, many needless divisions have remained and opportunities to create coordinated services have not always been grasped. The organizational environments of individual colleges have often impeded cross-college development, broad conceptual thinking or service development. This, however, may change, and a more unified pattern of operational frameworks may emerge as integrated learning resource provision becomes more accepted by principals.

The above assertion has to be defended. External pressures, commercial realities and the instinct for survival will drive colleges towards unified operational policies. The colleges' independent status and desire to survive and ensure access to further education students and the local community will be strong. Every element within a college will be examined as the realities of self-management become clear. The value of a service and its contribution to the organization will be assessed. The library will not be exempt from this; staff and the constituent parts of the service will be subject to scrutiny. For the librarian, this is an opportunity to put before the college the role the library can play and to show that it can help a college to achieve some of its main objectives.

The college may wish to increase the number of advanced courses it offers, develop more flexible courses and extend its range of special courses, all to increase market share and appeal. It may wish to extend its workshops to provide greater flexible learning opportunities, or to enter into agreements with adult education establishments and community initiatives. It may wish to increase its franchised courses, or franchise some of its own courses. Managers may have to ensure economic viability by reducing contact hours, while still maintaining academic standards. The library and learning resources services have a role to play in ensuring that the college can meet these aims. Libraries and other learning resources services will become, perhaps for the first time, important tools for senior managers to ensure that the college can respond to new initiatives.

Strong learning resources services help colleges to increase student numbers while maintaining quality. They assist departments to grow by giving students alternative environments in which to study; this in turn releases departmental resources and offers better space utilization. Enhanced learning resources can offer students a greater range of technical support and can assist the creative process. A strong, well-integrated service can offer the college a hard marketing base from which the college can appeal to potential students. The library and learning resources will no longer merely exist; they will in the front line of college development.

The days of the token library, media centre or IT unit are past. These services will have to grow and cope with more change than any other part of the college. Where many of these services have been closely allied to the needs of teaching staff, they must be opened out for student-centred access. This will require expensive and sophisticated hardware and will not be easy. There will be growth in open access computer suites for students, in reprographics shops, video centres, laboratories, workshops, language centres, educational advice centres, careers, personal and financial advice centres; all will become part of the new college environment and may well be grouped together into multi-purpose service points.

There may be a corresponding growth in the status, numbers, career opportunities and financial rewards for learning support staff. Such services will be a genuine career choice. In time, all learning resource and technician staff will be allied to the delivery of the curriculum and this, like the reduction in EC trade barriers, should allow for freedom of movement – in this case within the college and between departments. It does not follow that librarians will be the natural choice to head such operations, but they should not be slow in sowing the seed of that idea. If they cannot head the operation, then they must make certain that, within any such enlarged service, the spirit which has made college libraries so adaptable and flexible becomes a potent force.

Convergence is a word much associated with such amalgamations and it offers a useful concept that may assist in guiding the early stages of any new learning resources service.

The first aspect of convergence relates to technological development. In discussing the development of the resources centre concept, I have not referred to how technological change has facilitated that development. As machines have become more versatile and easy to use, so their absorption into resource centres has become easier and their management less problematic. The rich mixture now available is well known, but a change is taking place that will affect not only the technology, but also how services are offered and organized. Convergence relates to the joining together of what might have been thought of before as different technical disciplines.

Photocopiers can be linked to computer graphics packages to permit direct transfer from computer screen to hard copy. Photographs can be stored from a camera, then viewed instantly on discs and later fed into a computer for editing, enhancing and captioning. They can be printed by another computer, on campus or elsewhere. Video cameras can input directly into computers, the images can be manipulated using video editing machines and re-edited, and multiple copies can be printed using high speed colour photocopiers. Multi-media opportunities for bringing together images from many sources and manipulating them into packages and learning support resources will soon be commonplace. Direct dialling into distant information sources will enable students to tap into resource bases created by other institutions.

This technological convergence is made possible by computing technology and related communication technologies. To cope with these changes, the old barriers between reprographics, curriculum workshops, educational technology, media services, information technology, libraries and production units must be removed. Staff will move from one area to another as the technology becomes familiar. This is not to say that specialists will not exist. Staff may remain within named areas of the service, but there will be no barriers between the areas. Few will be appointed to learning resource services in the next few years who do not possess wide technical skills. Colleges will wish to gain maximum benefit from this movement to ensure that students can benefit. This is particularly important as the amount of time a student will spend in the formal teaching situation will be reduced.

This technological convergence will have to be matched by the second aspect – service convergence – which must be incorporated into new learning resource services to guide their development. I propose ten operational principles to govern this; some of these already operate within my own learning resource service.

1   The service has to work exclusively for the benefit of the students and all college staff. It must be an enabling service, supporting curriculum development, new teaching methods and experimentation. It must take a positive attitude in encouraging new thinking and in widening opportunities for everyone. It must be flexible, creative and innovative in respect of its external and internal organization.

2   Students and college staff must be free to move between all

sections of the service and find, as standard, the same level of support, quality of service and personal treatment.

3   The whole service will have shared aims and objectives, written so that they are applicable across the whole spectrum of the service, irrespective of its technical base.

4   Staff working within the service may be deployed throughout the service. Levels of skill will dictate the complexity of the tasks they will be asked to perform. No member of the service's staff will be denied the opportunity to acquire additional technical skills on any equipment provided within the service.

5   Within the service, all equipment, software and materials will be shared internally by the staff of the service, for the mutual benefit of the whole service and those who use it. Any item purchased for the development of the service will be common property within the service. Innovation within one part of the service can be rewarded and the results transferred to any other part of the service which may benefit from them.

6   Staff at any service point will direct enquirers to that part of the service which can assist them best. No artificial barriers will be created within the service which may inhibit its smooth operation or the services it provides.

7   All finances received from the college by the service will be common property within the service and will be applied to the best effect. Where the service can generate income from its own efforts, it should be able to retain that income for its own use. Income so generated is shared between the whole service and is not the property of those parts of the service capable of making income. Income may be spent in any way deemed necessary by the service; this includes hardware, software, staffing or the procurement of consultancy advice.

8   All facilities must be freely available to staff and students, or offered at cost price, as long as the commercial necessities of the college are not compromised. All or part of the service may be used to generate a profit for the college, or any company set up by the college, resources permitting.

9   All learning resource staff will have avenues of communication to the management of the service. Staff development opportunities will be shared and participated in by all in the service. Staff development will be so directed as to benefit the mission of the college, the development of the service, and the personal development of the individual staff member concerned.

10   The highest standard of quality of service achievable will prevail, consistent with the financial resources available, and will reflect the college's own definition of quality.

These ten principles embody what I believe to be the convergence theory of service. They may not meet with complete agreement; they include some difficult political and human problems. However, for college managers or librarians seeking to find some rationale for the reorganization of learning resources, they offer a starting point. The challenge is there for all colleges to survive; they must harness their strength in the interests of students. An underlying theme relating to resources centres is that they offer opportunity to place some resources directly in the hands of students. Within the new learning environment, more students will be given time to spend outside formal departmental territory. The decisions that librarians have made in the past relating to making materials, advice, hardware and software accessible to students represents a store of experience that should now come into its own. Experience and sense of service must be directly transferable to other parts of the college; this, together with the library, can provide a genuine learning environment for the twenty-first century.

Within technical and further education colleges, librarians have often been responsible for a greater range of resource service points than their professional colleagues in higher education. Within the context of the new further education, we should build upon that experience and enjoy the spectacle of higher education trying to catch up!

References

1   Whitworth, T. A., *The role of the technical college librarian*, Bradford University (MSc thesis), 1969.
2   Wright, G. H., *Technical library and information service in technical colleges*, Association of Technical Institutions, 1968.
3   Brewer, J. G., 'Towards a rationale for learning resources', *Learning resources journal*, **4** (3), (1988), 89-99.

Select bibliography

Beswick, N. W., 'The school library as a resource centre', *Library Association record*, **74** (8), 1972, 135-8, 140.
Bosworth, D. P., 'Stand up the real educational technology', *Learning resources journal*, **6** (2), (1990), 43-7.

Bradford, S., 'Audiovisual materials in the college library', McElroy, A. R. (ed.), *College librarianship*, Library Association, 1984.

Brown, J., 'Librarians and flexible learning', *Learning resources journal*, **7** (1), (1991), 16-19.

Button, B. and Hart, M., 'Changes in teaching and learning in higher education; the place of new information technology', *Computer education*, February 1992, 28-9.

Capewell, P., 'The enterprise approach in colleges: its implications for learning resources', *Learning resources journal*, **6** (3), (1990), 58-61.

Clarke, T., 'Creative teaching and learning', *NATFHE journal*, April-May 1991, 18-22.

Drodge, S., 'Learning resources management and change in further education', *Learning resources journal*, **5** (1), 1989, 2O-2.

Field, M., *Resourcing tomorrow's college*, Further Education Unit (Occasional Paper 1), 1992.

Gill, B. H., 'Educational technology in the academic library', *Programmed learning and educational technology*, **12** (3), 1975, 151-62.

Heery, M. J., 'AVM in academic libraries', *Audiovisual librarian*, **9** (4), 1983, 183-96.

Henry, T., 'The enterprise approach in further and higher education: the challenge to learning resources and flexible learning', *Learning resources journal*, **6** (1), 1990, 3-6.

Her Majesty's Inspectorate, *Core skills in further education*, HMI report 294/90/NS, 1990.

Holder, M. and Hewton, E. 'A school resources centre', *British journal of educational technology*, **4** (1), 1973, 41-53.

Jones, K. H., 'Creative library management; part two, the existential perspective', *Assistant librarian*, November 1973, 178-82.

The Library Association, *College libraries: recommended standards of library provision in colleges of technology and other establishments of further education*, Library Association, 2nd rev. edn., 1971.

Linkston, V., 'Establishing a learning resources centre', *Industrial training international*, December 1972, 360-2.

McElroy, A. R., (ed.), *College librarianship: the objectives and the practice*, Library Association, 1984.

Nazir, A., 'The use of computers in London colleges of FE', *CoFHE bulletin*, Spring 1979, 7-8.

Neal, K. W., *British academic libraries*, Neal, 1973.

Sands, T H. 'The development of a mathematics workshop'. *Learning Resources Development Group Bulletin*, 4, (1981), 17-18.

Scott, D., 'Technical support for learning development in the 90's: some issues', *Learning resources journal*, 6 (1), 1990, 7-11.

Shifrin, M., 'The library and information service at the ILEA's Media Resources Centre; a personal view', *Education libraries bulletin*, 53, Summer 1975, 21-30.

Shreeve, R., 'Minicomputers in FE colleges and secondary school libraries', *Learning Resources Development Group Bulletin*, 5, October 1981, 79.

Wyatt, H., 'A resources centre in geography teaching', *Geography*, 58 (3), 1973, 260-2.

5

The role of the librarian in student learning and assessment

Paula Kingston

Introduction

In the last decade, continuous and rapid change has been a feature of the education system, inspired by government policy and initiatives, new and changing curricula and the developing use of new technologies for learning. Together, these changes have major implications for the role of librarians in educational institutions. Many of the skills librarians possess are vital to developing students' learning skills and to providing and managing learning environments which enable students to develop autonomy in learning. Of fundamental importance to the recognition of the librarian's role in educational institutions - whether they be schools, colleges or universities - is the engagement of librarians with the curriculum and the learning process. One indicator of this is the extent to which librarians are involved in the assessment of learning.

As new emphases bring to the fore the skills needed to enable learners to learn, it is increasingly important for librarians to build on and further enhance their role in curriculum planning and development. Librarians have a major contribution to make, not only to the development of these learning skills, but also to their assessment. As will be seen later in this chapter, the assessment of skills - as opposed to knowledge - requires new techniques and approaches, which librarians are well placed to develop from the experience they already have of assisting people with the process of acquiring information skills.

Changes in teaching and learning styles, the increasing use of new technologies in the curriculum and in the management of learning, and the importance of improving access to learning through flexible approaches, are contributing to a time of unprecedented change and opportunity for librarians. A major challenge for librarians is to break down the often entrenched and stereotyped perceptions of their role; to continue to develop links and partnerships with teaching colleagues in planning programmes of learning; and to promote with confidence their role in enabling students to acquire, develop and apply information handling skills, in their broadest sense.

Developments in the curriculum

The 1980s and early 1990s have seen major and radical changes both in the infrastructure of the education system itself and in the structure, content and delivery of the curriculum. These changes run throughout the education system, affecting people of every age range; a common feature has been the shift of focus to the needs and attainments of the individual learner. A number of these changes and initiatives are outlined below to provide an insight into their cumulative effects on approaches to teaching and learning across the different sectors of education.

In the 1980s, the Business and Technology Education Council (BTEC) – established to promote and develop high quality, work-related courses – introduced modular approaches as a key feature of their courses. This brought with it the need to identify common skills areas, and a focus on student-centred and activity-based learning. The benefits of involving librarians as members of course planning teams in order to support assignment-based approaches rapidly became apparent, at least to librarians themselves, and many seized the opportunity to contribute to the planning and delivery of BTEC modular courses.

Similarly, the Certificate of Prevocational Education (CPVE), introduced in 1985 and aiming to help prepare students for the world of work, contained a major skills element. It consisted of three parts: a core, vocational studies and additional studies. The core had contained aims and objectives relating to the basic skills needed for adult and working life which were to be delivered, not as separate elements, but throughout the course.

Technical and Vocational Education Initiative

The Technical and Vocational Education Initiative (TVEI), funded by the Department of Employment, was introduced in schools in 1983, with the aim of encouraging the provision of technical and vocational education for young people. It began as a series of pilot projects to explore and test methods of organizing, managing and resourcing repeatable programmes of vocational education. In

1986, TVEI extension was announced, which enabled local education authorities (LEAs) which had undertaken projects to extend the principles of TVEI to all students between ages 14 and 18, both in schools and colleges. TVEI provided a major injection of resources into educational institutions, including accommodation, equipment – particularly computers – staff and in-service training.

Flexible learning approaches also became an issue within TVEI, as the implications of using new technologies, and of providing students with the skills required for the world of work, were addressed. A National Flexible Learning Programme was established in 1990 with two key objectives.

- To meet the learning needs of students as individuals and in groups through the flexible management and use of a range of learning activities, environments and resources.
- To give the student increasing responsibility for her/his own learning within a framework of appropriate support.

The benefits to students of this approach were seen to include the opportunity to develop learning skills, increased autonomy and responsibility for their own learning, the ability to work independently and/or as part of a team, and increased motivation. The flexible approaches to learning were explored within such initiatives as TVEI. They also had profound implications for teaching staff. They encouraged the development of teamwork across course and subject boundaries and they required teachers and lecturers to develop a wider range of teaching styles. Staff could no longer remain isolated in their classroom, but needed to work closely with other teaching colleagues and with librarians to meet the needs of students. This had the added advantage of facilitating institutions' responses to an increasing number of new educational initiatives, such as the national curriculum and core skills for the 16–19 age range. Teachers, lecturers and librarians were beginning to learn how to work together in planning and delivering programmes of study. Team and whole-institution planning would be increasingly a feature required of educational organizations, to enable them to respond effectively to change.

National curriculum
The school curriculum had already seen a major change prior to the national curriculum, with the introduction in 1986 of the General Certificate of Secondary Education (GCSE). This placed

increased emphasis on project-based approaches, requiring learners to use a range of resources, and entailed continuous assessment in the form of coursework, which contributed at least 20 per cent to the final mark. Shortly after the first intake for GCSE had completed their courses, the Education Reform Act of 1988 introduced a national curriculum for primary and secondary schools in England and Wales.

The national curriculum brought with it a more systematic approach to setting out the knowledge, skills and understanding required of learners at various stages and levels. It consisted of three core subjects, English, science and mathematics; and foundation subjects, including history, geography, technology, physical education and a modern foreign language. An important feature of the national curriculum was the introduction of attainment targets to establish what each pupil should be expected to know, understand and be able to do at the ages of 7, 11, 14 and 16. Individual pupils were to be assessed on whether they had met the attainment targets laid down, implying an increased focus on the needs of the individual learner.

National Vocational Qualifications

In the area of vocational education, a more structured and systematic approach was also being developed by the National Council for Vocational Qualifications (NCVQ), established in 1986 to reform the vocational qualification system. Each National Vocational Qualification (NVQ) was to be made up of separate units stating what an individual must do and to what standard. Each unit covered an area of competence and a level which placed it within the NVQ framework.

The emphasis was to be on the outcomes of learning, rather than inputs, and on ensuring that students could demonstrate competence in applying and using what they had learned, rather than demonstrating knowledge for its own sake. There was considerable controversy and debate on the meaning of competence and how it could be assessed, and fears of an increasing 'tick list' type of approach to assessment, which could fragment learning itself.

Open and flexible learning

Open and flexible approaches to learning have long been in evidence in the further education sector with initiatives in the 1980s such as FlexiStudy, the Open Tech and the Open College and the establishment of open learning centres in many colleges. In some of these initiatives, the emphasis has been on providing packages and an area where they can be used. Other initiatives have emphasized the importance of tutor support and helping students learn how to learn. However, in many cases these initiatives have remained on the periphery of the mainstream college curriculum, or have been integrated only because of the enthusiasm and dedication of individual members of staff.

More recently, there has been encouragement from central government to bring flexible learning into the mainstream in post-16 education and training. This is viewed by some as an attempt to reduce costs by cutting down on class contact time, while others are seizing the opportunity to implement a philosophy of student-centred learning, at the same time trying to ensure that the need for tutor support is highlighted and maintained as a legitimate part of lecturers' teaching hours. The NVQ initiative and the increasing emphasis on competition in the further education market, as well as the rapid expansion of student numbers, are fuelling the move towards flexibility in learning with its emphasis on meeting the needs of the individual student, and on removing restrictions on methods and periods of learning.

Rather than colleges offering set courses, starting at defined times, colleges are widening the range and nature of the learning opportunities they offer. Increasingly learners have the option of starting to study when it is convenient to them, of having their needs individually assessed and receiving accreditation for prior learning, and then having an individualized programme of learning developed for them. The implications of this model are an increasing need for modular training, for open learning opportunities, for access to computer-assisted learning (CAL) and for opportunities to engage in experiential learning. The need for increased flexibility of provision and resource-based approaches to learning is very much in evidence and publications such as the Further Education Unit's (FEU) *Flexible colleges*[1] provide a framework to assist colleges in increasing the flexibility of all aspects of their provision, both in the curriculum and in their institutional structures.

Core skills in the 16–19 curriculum

The need for students to develop a range of core or common skills, both to equip them for the world of work and to provide a base of skills for learning, was increasingly emphasized in the 1980s. BTEC and TVEI had already addressed this issue in defining common skills and developing the notion of curriculum entitlement, and further attention was focused on it in the late 1980s. In 1989, the report of the Confederation of British Industry's (CBI) Vocational Education and Training Task Force,[2] established in response to serious concerns about skills shortages, identified common learning outcomes the task force saw as requirements for working life. These included effective communication, the application of numeracy and information technology, personal and interpersonal skills, problem solving and positive attitudes to change.

In November 1989, the then education secretary asked the National Curriculum Council (NCC) to advise him on which 'core skills' should be incorporated into the study programmes of 16–19-year-olds taking A-levels, and to consider the implications for other students in the 16–19 age group. He also asked Schools Examination and Assessment Council (SEAC) to consider with NCC and others (NCVQ, FEU and the Training Agency) which of the core skills could be promoted through common requirements across all syllabuses and how they could be assessed, recorded and reported. The development of core skills across both A-level and vocational courses was seen as helping to bridge the academic/vocational divide, by providing transferable skills and accreditation. The NCC report[3] recommended that the following skills should be incorporated into the study programmes of 16–19-year-olds:

- communications
- problem solving
- personal skills
- numeracy
- information technology
- modern language competence.

They also stated that the five cross-curricular themes for the 5–16 curriculum should be extended post-16 to develop scientific and technological, aesthetic and creative, and social and economic understanding. These themes would provide a context for developing core skills.

The report recognized that all students should be entitled to guidance in their choice of options, to plan study programmes, review progress and prepare for the next stage of their careers. This should entail the development of individual action plans, regular assessment and progress reviews and reporting through records of achievement. Further work was needed to exemplify the assessment and reporting of core skills within post-16 syllabuses. SEAC, NCC, NCVQ, FEU and Training, Enterprise and Education Directorate (TEED) established a task force to undertake work on developing definitions, attainment targets and statements of attainment for the six core skills. Awarding bodies such as BTEC, City and Guilds and the Royal Society of Arts (RSA) began working to develop guidelines for core skills, including approaches to assessment.

However, the White Paper *Education and training for the 21st century*[4] left A-levels untouched, but introduced new combined academic and vocational diplomas and more general National Vocational Qualifications (GNVQ), not focused on a particular employment sector. Awarding bodies began work to incorporate these into their provision, offering them at different levels through both mandatory and optional units. A specified level of achievement has to be reached in three core skill areas of communication, numeracy and information technology, whilst others are recorded in the record of achievement. At Level 3, GNVQ has parity with A-levels and thus provides a route to higher education. Assessment is often assignment-based; for example, City and Guilds are building on their activity-based approaches, with students building up a portfolio of evidence which is judged against set criteria.

Information skills

As we have seen, throughout the 1980s and the early 1990s curriculum change increased the focus on the individual learner and on autonomy in learning. The emphasis on open and flexible approaches to learning and the acquisition of core skills by learners recognized that they needed both the skills for learning and the skills to enable them to operate effectively in the world of work. Many of these skills are encompassed within information skills in their widest sense.

Information handling skills have been defined and exemplified in a number of contexts, often building on the work of Michael Marland.[5] In a recent survey of information skills in further education by Markless,[6] these skills were defined as including library skills, study skills, cognitive skills of the type needed to handle information, and the additional skills needed for independent study, such as planning and prioritization skills.

In the context of assignment-based approaches, information

handling skills encompass defining what needs to be done, identifying appropriate sources of information, using these to retrieve the information required, and recording the relevant information. They also encompass such decisions as: interpreting the nature of the assignment, planning approaches to the task; deciding on the range of potentially useful sources of information; making judgements on the scope of each source, its particular emphasis or viewpoint as compared with other sources, and its accuracy and currency; selecting the most appropriate sources; using these efficiently and effectively through understanding their arrangement; organizing, interpreting and evaluating the information retrieved in the light of the assignment; applying the information to the task in hand; deciding on approaches to presentation; and, finally, reviewing the overall approaches and strategies adopted to complete the assignment.

These skills form a major strand of the professional competence of librarians which they can offer as a major contribution to curriculum planning and development. These skills also encompass many of the skills defined as core or common skills in post-16 curricula. Communication as a core skill includes identifying, retrieving, analysing and presenting information. Problem solving includes identifying the problem, analysing it, developing strategies to solve it and reviewing their success. Personal skills include the identification of preferred learning styles and developing skills to work as part of a team. Resource-based activities provide a vehicle for the development of all these skills, and library and learning resource centres can be seen as a natural base or starting point for acquiring them.

Similarly, information technology as a core skill requires that learners develop the skills to use and apply it. Libraries are increasingly centres where electronic media are used to access and manipulate information. Online catalogues, CD-ROMs, interactive multi-media resources and access to remote databases are examples of the information resources available. Libraries are also a natural base for providing access to generic information technology packages such as word-processing, spreadsheets and database software which students can use in conjunction with other information technology-based or printed sources of information as they work on projects and assignments.

Developments in information technology have increased the range and media of sources of information, and have increased the possibilities for access to and manipulation of information. But the point needs to be made that the information handling skills outlined above apply equally to using both information technology-based and other information resources. However, the specification of information technology as a core skill still appears to reflect a very narrow approach. In the context of information technology within TVEI, this problem was identified by Howard:[7] 'Students are exposed to the basic skills of computer use but that often becomes an end in itself. The use of the computer as a tool in a much wider process is often neglected. So too therefore are the skills associated with a more general approach to problem solving.'

Connections between information technology skills, and those of problem solving, communicating information and teamwork, are still not adequately perceived and understood; this is reflected in the development of separate modules for information technology as a core skill, rather than those skills being developed through other curriculum areas.

Integrating information skills into the curriculum

A number of barriers to the integration of information handling skills into the curriculum in the context of TVEI were identified by Howard.[8] These included a failure to adopt a 'common factor' approach, which is defined as analysing the common factors inherent in a number of curriculum innovations and focusing on these; for example, the common factor of student-centred learning across a range of initiatives. Also identified were a lack of appreciation and understanding of the concept of information skills as an essential part of a strategy for student-centred learning, and the lack of an infrastructure to accommodate them.

Howard points out that

Innovation in education is difficult at the best of times, cross-curriculum initiatives appear to be one of the most difficult to implement. In those situations where an infrastructure has been established there has usually been a clear direction from the senior management team, a clear model for development available to most teachers and departments, a highly visible and well-used library and/or resource centre, collaboration between and within departments and ongoing in-service to support the required changes in teaching style.

The complex set of conditions outlined here as essential to successful cross-curriculum innovation indicates why progress in developing whole-institution policies and approaches to information handling skills has been problematic. Two surveys, one conducted by Malley[9] and another by Markless[10] provide an insight into the current status of information skills in the further education sector. Malley's survey, focusing on the role of librarians in information skills, found that those taught by librarians lay largely within the area of traditional library skills. It indicated that prospects for a more widespread movement into wider skills were limited by low professional staffing levels in libraries, the fact that these areas were already the responsibility of academic staff in departments of liberal and general studies and so librarian's involvement might be seen as an encroachment and, lastly, that any moves for wider involvement might be seen as an attempt to alter the status of librarians.

Markless's survey focused in depth on information skills in 11 colleges. This project was undertaken in 1989 and 1990 and aimed to make recommendations on the future provision of information skills teaching and to describe strategies to support and encourage good practice. It found that the library was often seen as 'a separate entity', and that librarians were often not involved in course planning. However, there were some examples where this was not the case, and where librarians were actively seeking representation on course teams and securing a remit from senior management for developing the role of learning resources areas. Markless identifies the factors which seem to support success in the implementation of information skills work within colleges as: a clear understanding of the nature of information skills and the processes involved in their development; the need for a policy framework; staff development; and adequate resources for student assignments. Given the current rate of change and the pressures on colleges from a range of initiatives, the crucial point is made that: 'If information skills are seen as just another new initiative it may well be side-stepped.... In addition, developing students' skills is not an easy option. It takes time and can require lecturers and librarians to take on unfamiliar roles and learn new skills themselves.'

A further publication by Morrison and Markless[11] considers strategies for senior managers, lecturers and librarians to enhance information skills in further education. It provides ideas on the routes for the development of information handling skills and outlines the need for effective use of college librarians and the library in this approach. This most recent evidence indicates that there is still scope for considerable progress to be made in promoting information skills within the curriculum.

Assessment

A useful indicator of the extent to which librarians have integrated themselves into the process of curriculum planning and delivery is their degree of involvement in student assessment. Alongside changes in the curriculum have come changes in approaches to assessment. For example, the assessment of core skills under the NVQ model means assessing competence – that is, the application of skills. Included in this is the assessment of whether these skills can be applied in a range of contexts, that is, whether students can transfer them. To make these judgements, evidence has to be collected from observation of activities over a period of time.

John Cowan, in his address to the 1987 CoFHE conference,[12] stated:

> by concentrating on process rather than product, and on the ability to use knowledge rather than on the accumulation of knowledge, there is an implicit demand on the teacher and on the system to assess how people do things, rather than what they do . . . librarians must share in the task of finding acceptable methods of assessment, particularly in respect of those competencies with which they are directly concerned.

Given the nature of core skills as outlined above, there is clearly potential for librarians to become involved in assessment – particularly where project work is undertaken in the library and especially where connections have been made between core skills such as information technology, personal skills, problem solving and communication – and how these connections can be developed and demonstrated through approaches to assignments.

However, the case studies investigated by Markless[13] found that there was 'little systematic collaboration between lecturers and librarians over information skills teaching, assignment planning or course development'. They also found that students' skills were still more commonly assessed by looking at the final product of an assignment, although in some cases there were opportunities for students to reflect at the end on how they had approached the assignment. It is clear that, in order to assess whether students are applying skills efficiently and whether their skills are improving, ways need to be found of recording how students approach tasks, whether this is through human observation or video, or by the students keeping logs which themselves form part of the assessment process.

Librarians who are involved in planning programmes of learning are well placed to help ensure progression and continuity in the skills students develop, as well as to contribute to observing, assessing and recording students' progress. Barriers to achieving this integration may be at the level of individual librarians' perceptions of their role, but more often are a result of lack of adequate library staffing levels, lack of resources, and therefore lack of time to cultivate routes into the curriculum in order to develop this aspect of their work. However, unless librarians can raise awareness of their potential contribution and demonstrate the benefits of their involvement in the learning process, even if this is initially in the context of just one course or programme, then it is difficult to see how change can come about.

Partnerships in learning

Evidence already exists of the benefits to the curriculum of a well-resourced and well-staffed library and learning resources centre. It is clear that the role and status of librarians can differ enormously from college to college, but moves to flexible learning and assignment-based courses, together with issues such as college incorporation, are creating a climate of change and opportunity.

In order for colleges to respond to the curriculum and institutional changes outlined earlier in this chapter, mechanisms are needed for whole-college policy development; and for teaching staff, librarians, technicians and administrators to bring their skills jointly to the task of planning at whole-institution level; and for developing learning programmes. The ability to work as part of a team and to recognize and value each others' strengths and contribution is vital to achieving the above. This frequently entails a major change for all these categories of staff, who have often been assigned a very specific role, and who may be perceived as having very different levels of status and contribution within their institution.

Work has been undertaken by the National Council for Educational Technology (NCET) on the role and contribution of librarians to this team approach, examining the benefits to learners and learning of partnerships between librarians and teachers. Two reports have been published to date, the first in 1990 as part of a feasibility study for the Training Agency.[14] It outlines evidence of the benefits to resource-based learning of librarians' involvement in curriculum development groups and collaborative teaching. The second report, also produced by NCET for the Training Agency in 1990,[15] identifies some of the barriers to developing professional partnerships and makes recommendations in the areas of professional status of librarians, government policy on library provision, initial and in-service training of librarians and research and development work.

More recently, in 1991, NCET undertook a review of flexible learning in schools, commissioned by the Department of Education and Science (DES), in consultation with the Department of Employment.[16] The review was based on an analysis of the literature on flexible learning; it looked at difficulties and obstacles to implementation, and evidence of benefits and implications for the role of the teacher and for school management. Although the focus of this review was schools, many of the issues identified are reflected in the experience of colleges.

Barriers to implementation included the lack of student and teacher skills. For students, deficiencies were apparent in the areas of study skills, information skills and planning skills, while for teachers the areas included tutoring, negotiating with students, managing resources, and information skills. In addition, a third of the studies included in the review pointed to 'the significance of teamwork in the successful implementation of flexible learning'. Particular aspects included team teaching (34%), partnerships with librarians (32%) and technicians (24%). The report also identified a number of issues for school management, including the effective management of resources, the deployment and integration of information technology, innovative and appropriate staff deployment of teachers, librarians, technicians and clerical support; space utilization; and more creative timetabling.

The future of learning

It is unlikely that the pace of change in the field of education will decrease, and developments in the field of learning technologies will continue to have a major impact on educational institutions. We have seen that the use of information technology brings with it the need for flexible and efficient management of resources, flexible staffing and timetabling, and the creation and management of physical learning environments which provide access to a range of multi-media resources.

The technological changes currently underway include the use of multi-media interactive systems and technology-based courseware; increasingly portable technologies such as palm-top computers and hand-held devices; increased use of satellite, cable and video technologies to provide access to learning from home; and rapid growth in the use of computer-aided administration and management systems.

Already technologies such as CD-I (Compact Disc-Interactive) – with its ability to combine images, text, sound and video, operated through a user-friendly interface – have made inroads into the home computer market. When large numbers of learners have access to these technologies in the home, educational institutions will have to address such issues as how to manage learning that can occur in a number of locations, how to ensure equity of access to learning for those who do not have such technologies available at home, and how to assess learning which has taken place in this type of environment.

The ability to access such a wide range of resources will bring a shift in the balance of power between teacher and learner, highlighting further the need for educationalists to see themselves as managers and enablers of learning. The range of technologies currently available or under development will have a profound effect on the education system as a whole – including its structure, funding and accessibility – and will change the nature, or even existence, of educational institutions as we know them today. Information technology is also changing the content and order of the curriculum itself. The NCET is currently drawing together some key messages from the published literature on how information technology is likely to affect the curriculum of the future.[17] Access to large stores of information provided by information technology will increase the emphasis on information handling skills and the ability of the technology to process information will reduce routine tasks. Simulations will offer learning opportunities which might otherwise be considered as too difficult or dangerous to manage, and the opportunity to ask 'what if?' questions will allow learners to explore and test in ways too costly or time consuming without information technology.

The value and emphasis placed on subject knowledge compared with skills is also an issue highlighted by the developing use of information technology. There is an increasing need for learners to develop critical thinking skills in order to evaluate, interpret, apply and present information. In both learning-related and work-related contexts, individuals will need to be flexible and adaptable to continuous change and able to apply skills in new and changing contexts. There is already anecdotal evidence that information technology enables skills and concepts to be acquired more quickly, or at earlier stages, or in a different order from that previously assumed. NCET is currently investigating these issues and gathering information and evidence to help identify more precisely the nature of the impact of information technology on learning.

Conclusion

The changes outlined above present both a challenge and an opportunity to librarians, as they imply greater emphasis on the planning and management of learning and learning environments and on skills development. The opportunities for librarians to develop their role in curriculum planning and in managing the learning process are visible in ways not previously possible. As we have seen, their skills complement those of teaching, technical and administrative colleagues, and the willingness and ability of all these categories of staff to work together as a team will determine how quickly and effectively colleges adapt to new requirements and to changing patterns of learning in the future.

References

1 Further Education Unit, *Flexible colleges*, FEU, 1991.
2 Confederation of British Industry, *Towards a skills revolution: report of the vocational education and training task force*, CBI, 1989.
3 National Curriculum Council, *Core skills 16 to 19*, NCC, 1990.
4 Department of Education and Science, Department of Employment, Welsh Office, *Education and training for the 21st century*, Cm 1536, HMSO, 1991.
5 Marland, M., *Information skills in the secondary curriculum*, Schools Council Curriculum Bulletin No. 9, Methuen, 1981.
6 Markless, S., *et al.*, *Cultivating information skills in further education: eleven case studies*, Library and Information Research Report 86, British Library, 1992.
7 Howard, J. and Hopkins, D., *Information skills in TVEI and the role of the librarian*, British Library Research Paper 51,

BLR&DD, 1988.

8 *Ibid.*

9 Malley, I., *A survey of information skills teaching in colleges of further and higher education,* British Library Research Paper 10, BLR&DD, 1988.

10 Markless, *op. cit.*

11 Morrison, M. and Markless, S., *Enhancing information skills in further education: some strategies for senior managers, lecturers and librarians,* British Library Research Paper 99, BLR&DD, 1992.

12 Cowan, J., 'The role of the librarian in learner-centred learning', J Gordon Brewer(ed.), *Educational developments: the challenge to library and learning resource services. Papers presented at the joint annual study conference of CoFHE and the Education Librarians Group, Bath, 1987 (p1-10),* The Library Association, CoFHE Group, 1988.

13 Markless, *op. cit.*

14 National Council for Educational Technology, *Management of effective learning; professional partnerships between librarians and teachers in flexible learning.* NCET, 1990.

15 National Council for Educational Technology. *Developing partnerships between librarians and teachers in flexible learning,* NCET, 1990.

16 National Council for Educational Technology, *Review of flexible learning in schools (11-16),* NCET, 1992.

17 National Council for Educational Technology, *Future curriculum; educational technology school,* Internal NCET discussion document, 1992.

6

The support team approach

Marie Adams

It is important to clarify at the outset of this chapter that 'the support team approach' refers to all staff in an educational institution, working together as equal partners in support of the student in the learning process: lecturers, librarians, technicians and administrative personnel. It is necessary to make this clarification because one of the less attractive aspects of working in an educational institution is the division of staff into teaching and non-teaching or 'support', with its connotations of hierarchy and status. Library and learning resources staff have been particularly affected by this artificial boundary between groups of staff and their roles. In many institutions their training, skills and the work they do with students have not been recognized, nor fully utilized, simply because they fall within the 'support staff' category and thus outwith the traditional structure of curriculum delivery.

This division is being eroded of necessity by curriculum development, with its emphases on student-centred and flexible learning, and by economic pressures to reduce the amount of time the student spends in the classroom. We are in a phase of considerable opportunity for 'support staff' to consolidate their very real contribution to the learning process and for librarians to take a leading and proactive role in the development of the flexible college.

Teaching, non-teaching

'Non-teaching' is a neutral descriptor, that is, it relates to a member of staff who does not 'teach' or, rather, a member of staff who does not teach in a classroom with a regular class contact timetable and who is not employed on an academic salary scale and conditions of service. The more commonly used 'support staff' descriptor for those who do not 'teach' is much disliked by this author, as in its context it suggests a subservient role, one of supporting what teachers are doing, rather than one of supporting students.

However, these definitions of 'teaching' and 'support' have become blurred and are becoming irrelevant. The emphasis on the teacher teaching has been gradually changing to an emphasis on the teacher as a facilitator of learning, as a guide and support to the student. This has been encouraged by a developing educational philosophy which deems it more desirable and effective for the student to be an active learner, discovering by doing, than to be a passive listener, reliant on learning facts which quickly become out of date. Key themes are the ability of the student, or learner, to take responsibility for her/his own learning, to transfer skills and to keep up to date.

This philosophy is reiterated by the Further Education Unit (FEU) in one of the best and most complete publications on the 'whole college' approach to flexible learning to be published to date:[1]

> Flexible learning requires students to be active learners. There is an emphasis on the process of learning and the ability to learn, rather than on the acquisition of knowledge; an emphasis on problem solving, on the ability to interpret situations and to take the initiative, rather than on following fixed procedures in unvarying circumstances; on the ability to obtain, relate, consider and apply information rather than on learning facts. This active approach to learning is particularly appropriate in a world in which the capabilities and potential of information technology have led to a continuing explosion of information, which therefore needs to be accessed and intelligently used by individuals, rather than stored in the human memory.

It is not difficult to see the role of the library and learning resources staff in the active learning approach. It is not a new role, but one which has moved centre stage in the education process, alongside the role of the formerly predominant and leading players, the teachers, rather than in their shadow.

Curriculum development

Curriculum developments have been covered in more detail elsewhere in this book. It is sufficient here to point to two major influences: to the work of the Business and Technology Education Council (BTEC), which as two separate bodies in the late 1970s highlighted the assignment approach to learning, and particularly the cross-modular assignment; and to the development of flexible learning. These developments required staff to work together and for a team approach to be taken in developing curricular programmes, materials and facilities for students to work in self-study mode outside the classroom.

The BTEC approach opened the doors to librarians to become more actively and formally engaged in the delivery of the curriculum as part of course teams. Objectives within BTEC programmes included information handling skills. Who better to teach these skills than librarians? Students were directed to libraries to undertake assignment work, individually and in groups. Study and research skills were of the essence. Even where librarians were not formally teaching in classrooms, they had a key role to play in assisting students to find, select and use information appropriately, both within the college library and from external sources. However, while the role of the library was clearly important to the success of the BTEC approach, there was by no means universal inclusion of the librarian in assignment planning. Nor was there universal agreement upon and adoption of the standards of library provision which should be in place before a BTEC course was validated. Ensuing curriculum initiatives have adopted the active learning approach, but the relationship between the library and curriculum delivery has remained a distinctively local feature, very much influenced by the relationship between individual librarians and lecturers in any given college.

FlexiStudy, which was pioneered by Barnet College in association with the National Extension College in 1977, paved the way for a student-centred approach with an influence which has escaped few, if any, educational institutions in the country. It allowed students to work at their own pace, when and where they wished, with prepared learning materials and tutorial support, and with access to all the facilities of the institution with which they were enrolled, including the library. However, open learning centres which were set up to administer FlexiStudy programmes tended to be separate from libraries, even though the facilities being provided for open learners were similar to those being provided in libraries for mainstream students. There has been a similar trend with the most common expression of flexible learning provision in colleges, that of the workshop, developed within subject areas with little or no link with the library.

The student-centred and flexible learning approach is currently manifesting itself in the development of the flexible college, the aim of which is to give students, or learners, the opportunity to put together their own programmes of learning in order to achieve their goals, not those set down by the college, the traditional academic year, rigid course structures or the teacher. Hence the provision of educational guidance and counselling services, the Accreditation of Prior Learning/Achievement (APL/A), the modularization of courses and Credit Accumulation and Transfer Schemes (CATS). Higher education opportunity is becoming available through the local further education college with the introduction of franchising and other cooperative schemes between higher education and further education. Liaison between further education and schools is similarly expanding educational opportunity. Cooperation and partnership in education are key themes.

The economic focus

Further education is following higher education in experiencing pressure to increase student numbers without increasing costs. Reducing course hours, that is, the number of teaching hours a week in which a course programme is covered, is one means of addressing this problem. This can result in fewer teaching posts and/or lecturers being freed to teach more students, or to prepare study materials. However, fewer taught hours means that students have to complete more of their studies by self-study. This in turn means that more students will spend more hours in open access areas such as libraries and computer centres which are staffed predominantly by 'support staff'. An interesting contribution to the teaching/'support' debate has been made by the deputy principal of a large further education college. If, for example, course hours are reduced to 15 hours a week and students are required to study for 30 hours a week to complete course requirements, then for half of that time they are dependent on the assistance of 'support staff'. In such a situation, can lecturers continue to claim supremacy in the learning process?

The role of the library

It has been necessary to set briefly the institutional structure and curriculum contexts before considering more fully the role of the library in student-centred and flexible learning. The library in an educational institution does not exist in its own right, nor as a separate entity; it is, or should be, very much part of the parent institution, proactive in and responsive to the changes in the educational process. The main focus of the library is the support of students; it supports staff and management too, but serves predominantly the students of all levels and abilities and in all modes of study.

The nature of the development of the learning process and of information has required the library to embrace information in all its forms, print, audiovisual, information technology; to collect, extract and organize material that might once have been regarded as ephemera, in order to cater for wide-ranging demands of individual students pursuing their own choice of research; to get to grips with technology for housekeeping purposes and for information retrieval, from photocopiers to CD-ROM and beyond; and to create a variety of learning environments to suit the needs of individual and group work. Silent, book-only repositories are, or should be, a thing of the past. Self-learning packages, multi-media packs, worksheets, three-dimensional objects, computer networks, satellite television – all these are part of the modern educational library which hums with activity, whether it is still retaining the title of 'library' or adopting the name of 'learning resources centre'.

Of critical importance is the role of library and learning resources staff in facilitating students' access to these resources, not simply physical access in terms of long opening hours, but access through their knowledge and understanding of what is available, of how to select and use the information most appropriate for their needs and how to present it, structurally and in physical form. The most complete facilities with regard to opening hours, materials, equipment and study accommodation will fail to achieve the purpose of a library in an educational institution unless:

• there are staff of sufficient number and expertise to act as intermediaries between students and facilities;
• there is the closest of cooperation between teachers and librarians in the provision, dissemination and facilitation of students' use of resources, not as a bolt-on, but as an integral part of the learning programme.

Such provision requires partnership, a team approach, a blurring of roles, and for students to see staff other than their tutors as an integral part of their support team. These requirements have always obtained, but the flexible learning approach coupled with reduced hours – which emphasizes the self-study mode – demands partnership between teaching and 'support staff' if the quality of the student learning experience is to be maintained. This provides for supported self-study, which is particularly important where the younger students are concerned. They need to learn how to take responsibility for their own learning and to manage their time; to regard non-class contact time as working time, not social time; and to see libraries, workshops and computer rooms as essential parts of their learning process, not optional extras.

Librarians are perhaps more aware of these needs than the majority of their teaching colleagues because they have been at the sharp end of the ramifications of student-centred learning. These include the lack of forward planning with regard to the resources the students require, not just physical resources, but the necessary learning skills with which to undertake their assigned work; the timing of assignments and the behaviour of students outside the classroom and towards 'support staff'. It is not always appreciated that the library has to respond to every new course, every style of learning, every cooperative arrangement with external institutions and that all too often library staff learn of these only when confronted with students requiring help with a piece of coursework. Numbers of library and learning resources staff are comparatively few. Involvement in curriculum planning greatly assists the informed provision of the right resources in the right place and at the right time for the students, including tutorial support, whether given by a librarian or a lecturer.

The role of the librarian

It would be less than accurate to claim that college librarians everywhere are straining at the leash to work in partnership with their lecturer colleagues and that it is the lecturers who fail to see librarians as their equals in the educational process. Unfortunately, there are some librarians who are content to administer the library, to embrace all forms of information and the new technologies and yet fail to see their role extending beyond the library's doors. They will help students within the confines of the library, but will not seek interaction with the lecturers. They will participate in college initiatives if invited to do so, but do not seek that involvement proactively, nor initiate development in curriculum matters. This may be partly an attitudinal problem, a blinkered view of the role of the librarian, or it may be linked to the status problem. Librarians appointed to non-teaching posts are more handicapped than their Burnham librarian counterparts in right of access to the various fora in which curriculum matters are discussed. However, lack of confidence is also a factor: in skills, abilities, role and even concepts. Surely it is the lecturers who should lead in the curriculum? They are the experts.

Student-centred, flexible learning is still a comparatively new form of curriculum delivery, particularly in higher education. There are a few further education colleges which are well developed in terms of the flexible college as expressed by the FEU.[2] However, the majority have pockets of excellence with flexible learning yet to be embedded college-wide. Flexible learning is not well understood. It tends to be associated with packaged open learning, for example FlexiStudy and the Open University (OU), rather than being seen as a means of enabling students to learn flexibly through a variety of methods and experiences which focus on their needs. There are fears that it is a redundancy tool with the package replacing the tutor, whereas in fact tutorial support is a constant factor in this learning strategy if it is properly implemented and resourced, wherever and however a student is learning. The emphasis on teaching may be diminishing, but it is being replaced by an even more demanding emphasis on identifying students' learning needs, on the students' acquisition of learning skills, on time management and on negotiated study timetables. Some tutors do not care for the idea of dealing with students on a one-to-one basis; they prefer group teaching and to be in control. However, flexible learning integrated with mainstream provision does not negate group learning practice. It simply become one of the means of learning, not the sole means.

Developing the flexible learning approach requires knowledge of what information and learning resources are available. Prepared packages and materials may be usable as they stand, but always require tutor support. There is much scope for 'pick 'n' mix' from a variety of sources, including in-house written and produced material. Flexible learning is heavily resource-based, therefore it involves the organization of a wide range of resources and assessment of these resources. It entails dealing on a one-to-one basis with learners of all levels and abilities and at different stages of progress. In an open access or workshop situation, the facilitator will not have prior knowledge of the enquiries the student will make and s/he may not know the answer to every question, but may have to seek the help of a colleague.

All of these requirements are within the scope of the librarian's training and experience. They are perhaps taken so much for granted that librarians fail to perceive their relevance, or to realize that in fact they (librarians) have skills that many of their teaching colleagues are having to acquire. Lecturers are faced with fewer hours in which to deliver their course programmes. They have the option of trying to cram a quart into a pint pot, or of looking again at their programmes to see which component parts can be delivered by other means. Some parts will require formal teaching input, others can be covered by the use of supported self-study in workshops and open access areas, and others again through a self-study mode. Lecturers are also modularizing their programmes; that is, creating a series of self-contained components for which the student gains credit. There may be modules which are common across a range of courses; for example, study skills. It is not for the lecturer to struggle alone to redesign course programmes, every lecturer in the college undertaking similar research into what resources are available. It is not for the librarian to struggle alone to cope with the student exodus from the classroom; nor for the student to struggle alone to cope with an increasing self-study load. It is for the lecturer and librarian to work in partnership, each recognizing and acknowledging the other's skills, in support of the student.

Working in a team, however, requires much of the individual: trust, respect, communication, a sharing of resources and, most importantly, the relinquishment of supremacy and control. The latter applies not only to the lecturer with regard to the learning process, but to the librarian in the operation of the library. This is not easy to achieve. It is suggested that it is here that the librarian takes a leading and proactive role. There may be less scope now for the librarian to enter the classroom as the now-reduced course hours are regarded as a precious commodity. However, there is much scope for the lecturer to be in the library/learning resources centre to give subject support to students in non-class contact time, alongside the librarian giving study and research skills support, the media technicians giving materials preparation and presentation support, and the information technology technicians giving support in the use of information technology facilities. This apparently rigid description is given for reasons of clarity; in practice, in a truly integrated approach such lines of demarcation blur considerably as every member of staff will have a variety of knowledge and skills with which to help the student.

To encourage the lecturer to become part of this support team requires of the librarian the willingness to share actively knowledge of sources and materials, not simply to acquire and store them.

The National Council for Education Technology (NCET), for example, has information sheets, packs and staff development material on a wide range of educational developments including supported self-study and CD-ROM. The library should be a source of flexible learning materials, and should take the initiative in offering to duplicate, organize and integrate in-house produced and workshop materials and so to create an active learning resources centre in which the lecturer is involved as a visible alternative to classroom-based learning. With the librarians' knowledge of materials, they are in a position to recommend materials which can be put together as a learning pack, or included in modules. They can also act as liaison between lecturers preparing materials and modules to help to avoid duplication of effort. Achieving the support team approach is similar to the achievement of an integrated learning resources service as it entails bringing together people with different but complementary skills who previously have been used to a fair amount of autonomy in their work. Ownership and common aims are vital.

The active library

The active library movement in the early 1990s was the initiative, not of a librarian, but of an engineering lecturer, Martin Allen, on secondment from his college as an open learning development officer for the county of Somerset. He had set up an open learning engineering workshop and a more general learning workshop in his college, greatly assisted by the librarian. As he became involved in local meetings of college librarians in his open learning development work, he realized that the role of librarians generally was undervalued. He organized a series of residential workshops in 1990–1 which brought together librarians, lecturers, technicians *et al.*, with the following proposed aim, objectives and outcomes:

Aim:

> The development of college libraries as active learning resource centres.

Objectives:

> To build tutor support teams of librarians, lecturers, technicians and administrative staff
> To develop interesting study guides and materials for use in libraries.
> To establish a system for contact time to be credited to

libraries for tutor support staff.
To develop the library as a central support unit to other satellite and practical skills workshops.

Outcomes:
Libraries will become recognized by students as places where tutor support is always available.
Support teams will become accepted as normal practice with the library as a natural base and become part of the infrastructure of the curriculum and resource management system.
Satellite workshops will make more use of the library as an active resource centre without losing their departmental autonomy.

The impact of these workshops held in Somerset – which attracted participants from all over the United Kingdom and which spread to London, Essex and to a number of individual colleges and groups round the country – has been enormous. Librarians and technicians gained considerable confidence in their roles and abilities and lecturers understood better the desire of librarians to be part of the educational process and the role they could play. The workshop sessions, discussion and interaction were a microcosm of the partnerships in learning which could be achieved in every college. Very real and exciting development of active libraries has been witnessed in many colleges, mostly because a librarian took the initiative with management and teaching colleagues. The most common reaction from these librarians was surprise that their colleagues had agreed to their proposals so readily. As is so often the case, the library had not been deliberately ignored; its involvement simply had not been thought about. Now, as our colleges are seeking the way forward on flexible learning, the opportunity is there for the professional librarian to show the way, not in a spirit of empire building but in the spirit of the active library, one of partnership and a whole-college approach to the development and quality of new learning styles. It is interesting to note that within Somerset itself, all colleges have open learning workshops in conjunction with the library.

Qualities required

Whether librarians are able to influence curriculum development within their institutions depends very much on how they perceive their role and themselves and on the image they project to colleagues who are not themselves librarians.

The Library Association defines the role of the college librarian as information professional, educationalist and manager of resources.³ Librarians need to believe in and practise these three roles equally. Without a strong and visible interest in current developments in education, they cannot earn or maintain credibility in their institutions, or claim an equal role with their teaching colleagues. Managing the whole resource demands a vision for the role of the library in the institution and the ability to promote actively its development in line with the institution's objectives, for example as expressed in the college's strategic plan. Once again, it is not only a question of responding to these objectives, but of contributing to their formulation through the library's own strategic or development plan. If the librarian does not have a vision for the library, then it is unlikely that any other member of the institution will. By promoting an active learning centre requiring flexible learning facilities and tutor support for the students, the librarian is sowing the seed in the minds of all those, not least in senior management, who will read the development plan. There is a need to think on the large scale and in the long term, not just to meet immediate needs. Where is the institution going? What does it hope to achieve? What role can the library play in the achievement of these hopes and aspirations?

Belief in these roles implies a confidence in them. There is a tendency for college librarians to suffer from lack of confidence to step outside their librarianly role, often encouraged by their perceived low status within their institution. It is this author's experience that lack of confidence and feelings of isolation are not the prerogative of librarians, but are common to staff at all levels who are involved in and promoting an innovatory approach anywhere in an institution and at all levels. Progress is made by people with a like-minded approach, whether their label is management, teaching or support. When working closely with enthusiastic, like-minded people, labels are forgotten. If there is not the power to implement, there is always the opportunity to make friends with and influence the people who do have the power to implement. Individual lecturers belong to course teams, which in turn belong to faculties or boards of study, which in their turn are usually represented on the academic board and other institutional committees and working groups. Confidence in the role of the librarian as a professional, the equal of all, can be worn as a cloak over the lack of confidence a librarian may feel in her/himself. To have a different role does not mean to have a subservient or subordinate one.

In the smaller institution, unlike the lecturer who on the whole works with several other subject colleagues and within course teams, the librarian has few professional colleagues with whom to debate issues and test ideas. Support for the librarian must be sought outwith her/his institution. The Colleges of Further and Higher Education (CoFHE) Group of The Library Association provides such a support system, with a regional structure for local contact and an annual conference which enables debate on current issues in librarianship and education. All this assists in the development and broadcasting of a professional consensus. CoFHE has also produced for The Library Association a set of guidelines[4] which prescribe the quality of service an institution can expect from its library in return for a recommended level of resource provision. The Scottish Library Association, in partnership with the Scottish Library and Information Council (SLIC), has produced a similar set of guidelines for further education colleges in Scotland.[5] The Library Association and CoFHE have actively promoted the role of the library and librarian with many influential external bodies, not least Her Majesty's Inspectorate (HMI), the Higher Education Funding Council England (HEFC(E)), and the Further Education Funding Council (FEFC). The librarian in her/his institution is a representative of the profession and its values and can have confidence in pursuing aims and developments which are shared by like-minded professionals in a similar environment. All are members of the invisible college and have its resources and its backing to call upon.

It may seem unnecessary to list a user-orientated approach as a required quality for a college librarian. Reference has already been made to librarians who will give every assistance to a student within the library, but not see their role extending beyond the library's doors. A user in an educational institution is a student or member of staff engaged in the learning process, which is the prime purpose of the institution. Therefore, a user-orientated approach goes beyond dealing with individual enquiries. It is using the knowledge of what the user needs to influence the development of communication, learning styles and resource provision. Generally speaking, the neutral role of the librarian will encourage students and staff to share concerns which they feel unable to express elsewhere.

Without breaking confidentiality, the librarian is in a position to convey the general mood, concerns and wishes of the user body to those in a position to implement change.

A mind ever open to change and to a better or different way of doing things is essential. Nothing is accomplished once and for all. Nothing is more irritating or counter-productive than becoming entrenched in one way of doing things 'because they have always been done like that'. Education is a fast-changing sector and the opportunities for librarians are enormous. Never mind the problems of cataloguing and security tagging multi-media packs, loose-leaf materials and CD-ROMs, if by providing such items the library becomes a real learning centre at the heart of the learning process.

Tenacity is a highly desirable quality, together with a realistic approach as an organization person. It can take years to achieve, or even partly achieve, a vision. Judgement is required as to what the institution's financial resources can bear and what its readiness to embrace development is. But the seed must be sown. Progress can be made slowly or in huge leaps and bounds. The librarian must be ready not only to seize opportunity, but to look for that opportunity, whether by working with one lecturer or course team within the institution or on a working party, or by bidding for the various pockets of special funding which are increasingly available in addition to the main budget.

Having good interpersonal skills, that is, managing relationships between people well, is an overarching quality required in any service occupation. The ability to get alongside people – to understand their fears, pressures and constraints and to win their trust and respect – is essential to the development of the support team approach. It requires confidence in what is being promoted, but also humility in the sense of being able to listen to the ideas of others and to compromise, modify or change in order to achieve. Flexibility is a key requirement not only of educational provision, but of all education providers, including the librarian.

Conclusion

The vision of this chapter is of an active learning centre which meets the needs of the learner outside the classroom and which has the potential of a drop-in centre for the learner as an enrolled student or a member of the local community who has identified a resource/learning need – whether to learn a language, brush up on percentages or essay writing, or to use a computer to produce a CV.

It provides a complete support system, including availability of tutor support. It is a vision which may be rejected by librarians as unrealistic in terms of their accommodation, staffing, financial resources and attitudes within the institution, even their own. It has often been said by librarians with a low resource base that The Library Association's guidelines[5] are unrealistic. The reply to this is that librarians can only start from where they are in their own institution, and measure achievement against the progress that is made within that institution. Without promotion of the vision of the active learning centre, however, nothing can be achieved. The FEU, in promoting the learner-centred college over the course-based college, is careful to acknowledge that 'neither the course-based college nor the learner centred college exists as described but features of each can be found in most colleges'.[6] So it is that the features of an active learning centre can be found in most colleges It is a matter of drawing them together and creating a whole, in partnership.

It is a sound maxim to take solutions, not problems, to senior managers and in the current state of education a forward looking and enthusiastic approach is welcomed. It is within the scope of the librarian to offer a quality solution to the problems being encountered with the development of the flexible institution. The institution's acceptance and attendant investment cannot be guaranteed, but it behoves the librarian continually to make the case. If ever there was a time when the college librarian's learner-centred philosophy and skills were to the fore, it is now.

References

1   Further Education Unit, *Flexible colleges: access to learning and qualifications in further education. Part 1: Priorities for action*, FEU, 1991.
2   *Ibid.*
3   The Library Association, Colleges of Further and Higher Education Group, *Guidelines for college and polytechnic libraries*, 4th edn., The Library Association, 1990.
4   *Ibid.*
5   Scottish Library and Information Council and Scottish Library Association, *Libraries in Scottish further education colleges: standards for performance and resourcing*, SLIC, 1993.
5   The Library Association, Colleges of Further and Higher Education Group, *op. cit.*
6   Further Education Unit, *op. cit.*

7

The college librarian

Ken Watson and Tim Lomas

Introduction

What is the function of a college librarian? This chapter will explore
the role, parts of it evident, parts of it less readily recognized, that
the librarian plays in an further education and/or higher education
college in the 1990s, both in the library itself and in the institution
as a whole. It will consider the demands that the role makes upon
the individual, how these have changed, and the impact that this
role may have upon the academic and learning experiences of college staff and students. A tripartite approach will structure this
examination, exploring the librarian as manager, information professional and educationalist. We will refer frequently to further education, but the role we describe has also emerged from librarianship
in colleges of higher education and the former polytechnics.

It is significant that this chapter has two authors, and that one
is a further education college librarian, the other a former site
librarian within higher education. This may serve to remind readers that further education and higher education have many similarities when it comes to running libraries. 1994, the year of this
book's publication, is the Silver Jubilee year of the Colleges of
Further and Higher Education (CoFHE) Group of The Library
Association, and this particular two-author, two-sector approach
epitomizes CoFHE's activities and its approach to librarianship.
Some of CoFHE's members are chief librarians of small organizations, college librarians; others are drawn from large libraries with
large staffs, where responsibilities are less broad; others again lead
the library in larger institutions engaged partly or wholly in higher
education. A strength of CoFHE is that it can draw upon the different experiences of these various types of people and so develop a
broadly balanced picture of the college librarian.

This chapter will emphasize similarities between further education and higher education, rather than differences, believing the former to be more significant. Further education institutions typically have fewer students than higher education ones, smaller library collections and fewer staff to service these collections. But size may generate less of a difference than is often believed. Many multi-site higher education institutions have library service points resembling those of further education in size. Even a single site higher education library service point may be divided into separate units (e.g., a subject floor), each with a fair degree of autonomy, approximate in size to many further education libraries, and offering their staff a comparable professional and managerial challenge. Furthermore, the tasks involved in operating a large or a small library differ in scale, rather than in fundamentals.

Since April 1993, a further blurring of distinctions between further education and higher education has occurred. Like higher education, further education now operates in a corporate environment. Its libraries have become cost centres. The single line budget will arrive, sooner or later. Income generation and accurate costing of services will be expected. Formal quality control measures will be operated. All these features are common to both further education and higher education. Furthermore, higher education's franchising of courses is encouraging the introduction of higher education library service provision into further education colleges.

The Whitworth perspective

The development of college librarianship in the last 25 years owes a great debt to the work of Whitworth.[1,2] It is worthy of note that his first work was produced in the same year as CoFHE was established. He was therefore describing the environment and the aspirations that brought forth CoFHE. The impact of Whitworth's work when first published, and its evolutionary effect on libraries, are explored by Allen Armsby elsewhere in this book (Chapter Four), but it is necessary to re-examine certain key aspects here, as they underpin much of the present-day role of the college librarian.

Not himself a librarian, Whitworth investigated the role of the librarian of the then newly created further education colleges through the several media of sociology, education and librarianship. He postulated that college librarians opted for either an 'extended' role or a 'restricted' role. He described the extended role as one which aimed to increase the library's influence within the college. This might be done by engaging in, for instance, educational advisory activities. The restricted role would aim simply at providing a traditional 'access to books' service. He showed that the degree of job satisfaction and/or frustration experienced and recounted by his respondents depended substantially on the role chosen, with the extended role generally resulting in greater satisfaction, and greater use of the library.

Since the early 1970s, the extended role has been expected of all college librarians; this has been brought about by developments in educational philosophy, the professional volition of librarians and trends in education for librarianship. Academic developments have included the shift from teaching to learning. College libraries have become more the workshop than the warehouse. The college librarian is a learning facilitator. Education for librarianship has been geared to increasing professional competence and confidence, exploiting as well as creating library collections, seeking wider facilitating opportunities and welcoming examination of performance. Many college librarians have sought this actively. Some few have responded negatively, but most have felt able and willing to meet the challenge of this extended role.

For Whitworth, the extended role had college librarians perceiving the library as central to educational activity. Library functions that supported this centrality were emphasized by the librarian. Amongst these would be user education, which it was hoped would lead to increased use and heightened appreciation of the library and its potential. The restricted role operated when librarians provided only an 'access to books' service, rather than seeing the library as a centre for educational development. Whitworth's findings have been expressed in recent literature in a shorthand manner by referring to 'proactive' (extended role) and 'reactive' (limited role) approaches to library service.

Whitworth also identified some of the frustrations and problems faced by those taking the extended role. There was some lack of appreciation of their stance by academic staff and students, and institutions frequently failed, or were unable, to provide enough space, staff or equipment. Problems about numbers of staff were, and still are, exacerbated by inadequate staff structures, often imposed from outside the library, and sometimes from outside the college. Many such structures seemed to be based on the premise that any pair of hands working in the library could address all the tasks requiring attention, irrespective of level or professional difficulty. However, there has been a gradual recognition by institutions of the need for an increase in library staffing levels and for improved structures. Encouraged by The Library Association, individual librarians, and the demands of changing educational patterns and philosophies, more staff have been employed in libraries. This has enabled librarians, in theory at least, to concentrate more upon the professional aspects of their roles.

Whitworth, as well as listing the problems and frustrations of the extended role, identified many positive aspects. These included job satisfaction in providing a lively service, considerable autonomy in operation, and a positive role in the policy-making and academic decision-making of the institution as a whole. He also looked to the future. He anticipated libraries increasing in size and importance. He foresaw the creation of learning resource centres and the tension that could arise between support services and academic services. He envisaged more women being appointed as college librarians. In 1992, 71 per cent of those in charge of further education college libraries were women,[3] compared with only 37 per cent when Whitworth wrote in 1969.[4]

Whitworth believed that the 'local nature of control ... will tend to militate against the implementation of standard conditions of service ... and uniform standards of library provision'.[5] Incorporation has emphasised such local control. Planning and strategy formation is more management led. The opportunity for decision-making after reasoned debate within academic boards is curtailed for a variety of reasons, not all to do with time constraints. The board of governors, now with less representation from an institution's members, and the Further Education Funding Council (FEFC) establish the principal unequivocally as chief executive of the college, as well as academic leader. There is considerable pressure to ignore external professional guidelines and subordinate them to perceived local need.

On the other hand, it is also true that college principals are keenly aware of their responsibilities as chief executives, and demonstrate a wish to take expert professional advice into consideration in their decision-making, provided they have confidence in the quality and impartiality of that advice. The recent Scottish exercise in developing standards for college libraries,[6] using a working group representative of all sectors of further education rather than simply a group of librarians, may point a lesson.

Since CoFHE first started developing standards and guidelines for college libraries on behalf of its parent body, The Library

Association, many of the points made by Whitworth have been addressed. The current fourth edition states, in effect, that the extended role of librarian described by Whitworth is now the expected norm: 'The better the links between the library and the institution, the more the library staff understand and identify with corporate aims, and the closer their involvement in debate and decision-making, the better the library can serve the institution.'[7]

For hard-pressed senior college management, this might come as a welcome revelation. For the toiling college librarian, it acts as a reminder of the demanding job that s/he is undertaking. The rest of this chapter will focus upon the taxonomy of the college librarian's tasks as proposed by CoFHE's *Guidelines*.[8] There, tasks are defined which demonstrate that the present-day college librarian needs to operate as a manager and an educationalist, in addition to filling the traditional role of librarian.

The college librarian as manager

The scale of management concerns obviously differs from college to college, partly with the size of the institution, but more significantly with the manner in which the library is established within the whole college. 50 per cent of libraries are autonomous units. 17 per cent have been merged or – in the preferred terminology – converged, within the last three years; such mergers have commonly involved the library, audio-visual units and computer services in single or multiple combination. 23 per cent are already part of such a larger learning resources unit. A number of these converged services might have an overall manager who is not a librarian, but librarians are normally responsible for the activity and plant within the library itself in such merged services.

There has always been at least a tacit acknowledgement that managing and developing stock, physical care of the collections, providing a catalogue, organizing the staff rota, providing audiovisual equipment and monitoring students' behaviour in the library are all part of the college librarian's brief. All these need 'managing' as well as 'doing'. The college librarian is the manager of: a capital resource (the stock and other plant); accommodation; people (staff, clients); technology (audiovisual material, computers, security system); finance (the annual budget); a service function (lending, retrieving information); and learning (the client activity facilitated by the smooth running of the library). For each of these, there is a range of managerial functions sitting along an axis running from the strategic to the operational. Educational changes have increased that range, which now places heavy demands upon the college librarian, and have tended to emphasize the 'managerial' over the 'librarianly', moving issues along the axis towards the strategic and away from the purely operational. Below, we attempt to illustrate the range and focus on aspects of the managerial role.

Libraries now house a wide range of equipment in addition to the collections themselves. We will not repeat the range of equipment listed recently by CoFHE;[9] it is enough to mention automated library systems, networks, computers, CD-ROM systems and on-line information retrieval facilities. The developments implied by the introduction of such equipment have meant expansion of the librarian's tasks. In addition to understanding its function in the learning process, there is a requirement to operate the equipment efficiently and to train both staff and clients how to make best use of it. Not everyone feels comfortable with the electronic age. Careful and detailed planning of the introduction of, say, a multi-function photocopier, or an OPAC, is essential, and demanding. This involves both staff development and the challenge of the management of change. We return to this below, in a section on staff development.

Not least of the college librarian's management concerns is finance. One commentator, reviewing the management challenges facing librarians, stated that the challenges are such that ' few have an opportunity to forget for long: they are routinely and acutely reminded of them with every new budget print-out'.[10] In the past, of course, librarians have always been expected to oversee their cash allocation. This has ranged from being given a single lump sum along with a 'please spend' request to highly constrained budgets, with detailed allocations to academic departments, determined in whole or in part outside the library, and based on formulae, the loudest voice, and/or gut reaction! The financial demands placed upon the librarian today are more sophisticated.

Institutions, given more financial independence, are gradually delegating elements of that independence to newly-designated internal cost centres. The college librarian's financial role includes the distribution of money under several budget heads: journals, the book fund, electronic information access, equipment, maintenance and others. A result of financial devolution has been to add further, more complex budget heads such as physical running costs, overheads and staffing. In general, the trend is for the librarian to be given more autonomy and scope for the application of a more broadly based library budget. This professional freedom is to be welcomed and should result in better informed expenditure on libraries, but it makes more demands upon the librarian. To create equitable budget heads from a single line budget requires considerable financial acumen, as well as a sympathetic understanding of institutional plans and needs, and of trends within librarianship itself.

The financial ethic of the recent past, not only in libraries, was the 'historic' budget - last year's amount, plus inflation (plus, given a good case and some good fortune, a little more!). Sometimes, the college librarian would be presented with an arbitrary amount, with no invitation to bid competitively, or to consult as to the amount's adequacy. Neither of these approaches is now acceptable. In their place comes the sensible requirement for stringent financial planning linked to defined objectives, service targets and business plans.

Such planning is, or should be, based on reasonably accurate costings. For this, some operational research is required, as libraries have perhaps too rarely costed their services. What does it cost to order and catalogue a book? What does it cost to maintain a video collection, bearing in mind off-air requests and licences? What does it cost to purchase a new journal, to make space for it and to check it in? These are all proper questions. They imply a need for time, and financial skills. Work has to be done to reach true costs, even though the costing is itself costly and time consuming, and requires special skills. But 'What does it cost to cost things?' is a real and legitimate question, no matter how clear the long-term cost-benefit may be, if no expert advice or personnel resources are available for the initial exercise.

Negotiating skills are essential, and not just for presenting and arguing a case before the senior management team. Of vital importance is the liaison with academic departments so that the library's business plan takes cognizance of other sectors' planning, and vice versa. This might have to consider new types of learning materials, additional study space, more project work or greater technical support. All of this has an impact upon the library physically, as well as calling upon its capital, revenue and human resources. No longer can the library afford to operate in a resource vacuum, concerned, say, to automate stock circulation, or increase shelving, simply because the library itself needs such work. Deliberation with other college sectors requires that the library, as a central service, coordinates its own specialist planning with that of other sectors of the institution so that the college as a whole may provide students with an all-round, considered learning experience.

Staff and personnel management skills, and an understanding of the management of change, are important tools in the armoury of the librarian as manager. Given the degree and pace of change (e.g., the rate of introduction of new equipment), there is a need to motivate staff, to encourage and make available both staff development in the widest sense and task-specific training. And there is a need to monitor effectiveness. Communication channels that are both workable and working have to be set up and maintained. Such channels need both to address everyday situations and to prepare for such major changes as incorporation and the installation of an automated system.

The staff of a library may include a range of grades (e.g., qualified librarians, library assistants, clerical assistants, technicians) and employment patterns (e.g., full-time, part-time, job share, term time only). An obvious operational task is to construct a rota while juggling the varied employment patterns. But more is involved for the college librarian than simply the creation of a rota giving optimum cover at busy times, or ensuring that annual leave is fairly handled. Tasks must be apportioned with regard to ability. Colleagues must be motivated, encouraged and helped to meet service targets. And this must be achieved within a climate that encourages positive and sensitive staff appraisal.

The college librarian as librarian
Over the last 25 years, the college librarian has striven after Whitworth's extended role, and has been supported in doing so by the professional consensus in librarianship and by trends and developing philosophies in education itself, not least the continuing shift from teaching towards learning. If the acquisition and application of managerial skills have been required, so too have been changes in the core professional expertise of librarians.

Bibliographic skills - knowledge of and access to an ever-expanding body of recorded information - are necessary. These have always been the centre of librarianship, but have increasingly involved seeking the advantages inherent in inter-institutional cooperation and the use of information technology. Moreover, the stock that clients now expect to find in a library is no longer restricted to the neat packages of journal or book. Collections of photocopied articles (within copyright constraints!), files of news-paper clippings, company reports, and much more, have appeared. A widening range of audio-visual material, and of computer soft-ware and its explanatory handbooks is also to be found.

The impact of information technology on the college librarian can hardly be overstated. Information technology applications are available not only for information retrieval but also for library housekeeping. Keeping abreast of developments, appraising the encomiums of sales people, making sound decisions on choice of system, even creating an in-house system, have all been added to the librarian's lot. Information technology has enhanced service quality (speed of transactions, efficiency) and aims at increasing service capacity and the range of information accessible. All auto-mated issue systems should be capable of delivering management information to show how a collection is being utilized and to assist in improving its use. The raw data thus produced need analysis using managerial and statistical skills to achieve results.

Information retrieval via information technology has come within the reach of most libraries, often through the medium of CD-ROM. But with this development has come the complex issue of how to spend the budget. Traditionally, the library budget has been used for collection building. Now the picture is less clear, for access to information via information technology is not free. The dilemma is: buy a couple of new journals or buy access to comput-erized databases, CD-ROM or online? The first adds to the long-term capital stock of the library, the second provides required information today. Acquisition on a narrow front? Or access on a broad one? Resolving this, and coping with the variety of search strategies that competing systems demand, have become part of the college librarian's task.

Libraries now house increasing numbers of Computer-assisted learning (CAL) packages. This application of information technol-ogy changes markedly one function of the college librarian. With a print-only collection, help has been expected by library users, either because of the users' special educational needs, or because assis-tance is needed in finding information. CAL has made the librari-an more frequently an intermediary in the actual learning process because when the CAL package is being studied, the library is open, the librarian is present, but the writer of the package is absent. By default, help – and the human contact – is sought.

Information technology has caused the physical nature of the college library to change. Networking, PCs for clients and automated issue systems have changed ideas on layout. With differing formats come the requirements of housing and displaying them. Their exploitation, often by electronic means, has to take place in the library and this has its impact on space utilization, let alone electrical sockets! Other physical changes have resulted from changing educational policies and the creation of learning resource centres and drop-in workshops, as described by Allen Armsby in Chapter Four. Increasing student numbers and new approaches to learning have increased demand for library services. These approaches manifest themselves by more self-directed learning, away from the classroom, utilizing library resources. The services include room for study, another aspect that physical planning has to take note of, and that study can be group or individual. Both of these need different work environments.

Provision of adequate stock remains a primary major library service. Stock has been put under great pressure by increasing student numbers. Decisions are required on numbers of copies per title, a variety of loan types to match sometimes eccentric patterns of course attendance and the need for popular items to move quickly from client to client. One outcome of this pressure is greater concern to conserve and repair existing stock. Another is the addition of security systems to library hardware. Clients trapped in these have to be faced, and the guilty winnowed from the careless and the mistaken - interpersonal and interviewing skills!

The college librarian as educationalist

The coincidence of increased student numbers resulting from government policies, and the general shift in emphasis and practice throughout education from teaching towards learning, have emphasized the centrality of library resources and their use, even if this has often occurred more by default and the belated recognition of changes in student needs and work habits than by conscious planning. They have also required the librarian to develop and apply (if s/he had not already done so) an intimate knowledge of educational policy and practice; it is now widely agreed that the concept of the librarian as simply a provider of books is outdated though, admittedly, there are still those outside the profession who perceive this to be the role.

The title 'tutor librarian' was, until recently, relatively common and indicated the college librarian's educational task. The title is now less fashionable; in 1992, only 16 per cent held the title,[11] against 42 per cent in 1969.[12] However, although the proportion of people entitled 'tutor librarian' has fallen, the proportion of titles indicating an educational role for the librarian (i.e., Whitworth's 'extended role') has held its own.[13] The impact made by librarians bearing the title 'tutor librarian' on the educational environment of colleges has permitted the modern generation of college librarians to continue, and increase, their input to the total learning experience provided by their institutions.

Whitworth wrote during the boom time of user education development. For tutor librarians, this aspect of the job was, rightly, high on the agenda. When Whitworth wrote, few in colleges – students, staff or management – fully appreciated what resources existed or how they could best be exploited to help people to function more effectively as learners, teachers or managers.[14] Librarians have mounted programmes of user education going well beyond a preliminary induction session, with varying degrees of success. User education is more than just finding one's way around a library and demonstrating sources of information and how to use them. It is aimed at giving lifelong and transferable skills to a workforce that needs to keep abreast of new information, and has the skills necessary to survive and prosper in an information-based, post-industrial society. But the librarian's input to the education of students has been greater than this de-mystifying of certain aspects of the librarian's own professional knowledge. Many college librarians have taught wider aspects of information and study skills, from how to create accurate bibliographies to strategies for literature searching. Such strategies demand substantial intellectual effort and a sympathetic understanding of the student's broader academic aims and whole work programme.

User education is only part of the educational contribution of college librarians. Michael Rowarth and Allen Armsby expand (Chapters Two and Four) upon the role of the college librarian as educational facilitator. The librarian is now to be found in the front line, providing tutorial support for student-centred learning and drop-in workshops. Even students 'undergoing' a more traditional learning experience can expect and receive tutorial help on understanding assignments set by academic colleagues. Librarians may be more easily found than lecturers!

The nature of the library as a centre for information gathering and a depository for information helps the librarian to keep abreast of educational developments. Its role as a central point in the college, serving people from all departments and levels, means that librarians are well informed about college trends, plans and initiatives. This knowledge has resulted in the positions achieved by many college librarians on academic policy committees, whose work can range across academic boards to course planning, validation and review committees. Occupying the middle ground gives the college librarian a cross-college perspective, a clear idea of how the learning process within the college is being achieved and, often, a perceived neutrality and impartiality of view amidst the welter of a college's inter-departmental manoeuvring!

Staff development

The college librarian has a complex task. Before concluding this chapter it would be useful to explore one aspect that brings together the three facets of the role described above - staff development. The librarian as manager initiates and facilitates staff development for library staff. In the qualified librarian and educationalist modes, the librarian is aware of her/his own staff development needs. These modes imply a willingness to contribute to the college's total staff development programme. The Library Association, in its *Code of professional conduct*,[15] requires its members to engage in continuing professional development.

Greater numbers of staff and the increasing sophistication of library activities demand the provision and management of training. Too often, this has had to be achieved without adequate recourse to a college training budget, which may have been reserved, historically, for 'teaching staff'. This, along with the difficulty of releasing colleagues from a sparsely staffed library service point, has been an impediment to staff development. However, these resource and procedural difficulties must be tackled if the library is to prosper and offer a proper service to the college.

The Library Association has developed guidelines[16] to assist members and their employers plot and record staff development needs and achievements. As these guidelines deal ably with the general staff development issues in further education and higher education libraries, it is the intention here to concentrate on the issues relating to the achievement of a learning resource centre and support team approach; that is, the requirements of the extended role.

The term 'librarian' in this chapter refers primarily to the (chief) college librarian. However, the staff development approach advocated is required of all library and learning resources staff: a willingness to work together with each other and other institutional colleagues in support of students. In the smaller further education college, the college librarian may be the only professional member of library staff. In larger further education colleges and in higher education, there will be other librarians or senior colleagues who share management responsibilities with the chief librarian or head of learning resources and who lead teams of staff. These shared responsibilities include setting the example by implementing a team approach within the service as well as promoting it in the wider environs of the institution; they also include identifying staff development needs, not only for themselves, but also for those for whom they are responsible.

With regard to library and learning resources staff development and the college librarian's own self-development, the following suggestions are made regarding the skills which may have to be acquired to achieve the active library and support team approach. They are clearly not exhaustive.

- Personal skills: interpersonal skills, assertiveness, customer care.
- Information professional: information technology and its applications; the use, production and management of flexible learning materials; copyright.
- Educationalist: the flexible college; teaching and learning styles; current education initiatives, for example, modularization; core skills; franchising; NVQs.
- Manager of resources: financial management; personnel management; building planning and design, including signing, health and safety; security; special needs considerations.

Staff development relates not only to library or learning resource staff, but to all members of the institution. The librarian can be involved in providing staff development for other members of the college; here, the librarian also has prime opportunity to communicate the library's role. Library and learning resources teams can invite representatives of course teams, or cross-college coordinators to discuss with them at termly or end-of-year meetings issues arising from the development of learning styles. Library staff can run in-house courses open to all members of the institution, or join with teaching colleagues in offering a programme on, for example, the student-centred approach, both internally and as an external, income-generating course. A user education programme offered by library staff to teaching and other colleagues may be a useful way of enlightening colleagues about the potential of the library and its staff. Contributions can be made to induction programmes for new staff and for governors. There is much to be gained from arranging a visit to another institution which is a good example of the integrated approach and inviting a lecturer or senior management colleague along. Inviting a lecturer or senior management colleague to contribute to a librarians' conference or publication is valuable; so too is accepting invitations for library/learning resources staff to make similar contributions to educational conferences and publications. The institutional or departmental newsletter is another means of raising awareness of the library's role or selling the dream. The proactive approach cannot be over-emphasized.

Staff development can be gained from in-house and external sources and where appropriate should be undertaken with other members of the institution to forge the common purpose and aims. It is not simply a matter of being aware of courses being provided, but of requesting appropriate staff development activities and initiating them.

Conclusion

Major changes continue to face the college librarian: the changing curriculum (franchised courses, General National Vocation Qualification (GNVQs)); new ways of delivering the curriculum (distance learning, drop-in centres); new types of student (special needs, mature); more students, of all types; new professional tools (electronic databases and bulletin boards).

'The modern library sits at the centre of all this', writes Tom Burness, a college principal, introducing the Scottish college library standards.[17] Thus, the college librarian is faced with a challenge and an opportunity. With managerial skills and the expertise of a continually developing professional, and as a knowledgeable educational practitioner, the college librarian is well situated for a varied, central and demanding role. Some institutions already acknowledge this and appoint and empower their librarian accordingly. Some still need to be reached or persuaded. Librarians already in post need to be active in publicizing their skills. Would-be college librarians need to be aware of the variety and importance of their future role. The future role of the librarian in academic libraries will depend upon how well we face the challenge of sharing responsibility for educating our students.

References

1 Whitworth, T. A., *The role of the technical college librarian*, Bradford University (MSc thesis), 1969.
2 Whitworth, T. A., *The college librarian: a study in orientation and role congruence*, Sheffield University (MA thesis), 1974.
3 CoFHE Group, Survey of FE college libraries in England, 1992 (unpublished).
4 Whitworth, *The college librarian, op. cit.*
5 *Ibid.*
6 Scottish Library and Information Council and Scottish Library Association, *Libraries in Scottish further education colleges: standards for performance and resourcing*, SLIC, 1993.
7 The Library Association, *Guidelines for college and polytechnic libraries*, 4th edn., Library Association Publishing, 1990.
8 *Ibid.*
9 The Library Association, Colleges of Further and Higher Education Group, *Guidelines to guidelines: a librarian's companion to The Library Association's Guidelines for college and polytechnic libraries*, The Library Association, 1990.
10 Moffett, W. A., 'Don't shelve your college librarian', *Educational record*, **63**, Summer 1982, 46-50.
11 Colleges of Further and Higher Education Group, *Survey of FE college libraries, op. cit.*
12 Whitworth, *The role of the technical college librarian, op. cit.*
13 Colleges of Further and Higher Education Group, *Survey of FE college libraries, op. cit.*
14 Fleury, B. E., 'Lectures, textbooks and the college librarian', *Improving college and university teaching*, **32**, 1984, 103-6.
15 The Library Association, *Code of professional conduct*, The Library Association yearbook, 1993, 162-3.
16 The Library Association, *The framework for continuing professional development; your personal profile*, Library Association, 1992.
17 Scottish Library and Information Council and Scottish Library Association, *op. cit.*

8

Quality in college libraries

Rennie McElroy

Introduction

This chapter considers where quality lies in college librarianship:
how college librarians seek to bring quality to their library services
and try, through the library, to add to the quality of the college as
a whole. To clarify the organizational context, I refer the reader to
the definition of 'college' expressed in the preface, for this chapter
is intended to address all of the types of institution mentioned
there.

Quality is the touchstone of the 1990s. It is on everyone's lips,
everyone's desk. Quality assessment, quality assurance, quality
audit, quality management (total and, presumably, partial!), quality
profile, quality provision. The concept of quality has a high profile. It is of strategic importance to educational institutions that
they be seen to be of high quality. The activity of measuring and
comparing quality in and between institutions from the outside (or
at least, claiming to do so) is a growth industry. But is the novelty
implied by all this activity and debate real, or spurious? Was there
quality before incorporation? Was there quality before quality
audit? For our immediate purpose: could quality emerge from college libraries, so often said to be under-resourced, with small collections and inadequate staffing, before BS5750 and TQM? If so, how
did this come about?

First, a disclaimer. There is a thriving industry devoted to creating definitions of quality and it has its own equally thriving literature. I do not propose to enter that industry or add to that literature in this chapter. It is not my purpose to debate the relative mer-
its of some or any of the many definitions of quality, support any
one school of thought, or create a new definition or a new school.
Colleges and their libraries have been characterized by pragmatism;
a pragmatic and widely accepted definition of quality is 'fitness for

purpose'. If beauty is in the eye of the beholder, then quality is in the perception of the manager (the librarian) and the experience of the client (the reader).

Fitness for purpose is closely related to other concepts: using resources well; generating more, rather than less, use of such resources; doing well that which one can do; doing the right thing, as well as doing things right; in a service function such as libraries, satisfying clients; being as sensitive to the needs of the client as to the 'traditional' practices of the profession. In college terms, this emphasizes responsiveness and understanding the whole-college view of priorities, as well as pursuing personal professional specialisms.

Influences on quality

Four factors have exercised great influence upon the manner in which college libraries have operated and the means by which college librarians have sought to deliver a quality service to their institutions.

First is the evidence of numerous surveys, undertaken over many years, that few college libraries enjoy great wealth of resource, whether in size of collection, numbers of staff, extent of accommodation, or funding. 'Adequate' and 'appropriate' are the terms commonly applied, because the system is coping – if only just – or to promote the concept of cost efficiency, or as weasel words, to divert attention from under-provision. Even during the resources honeymoon of the late 1960s and early 1970s, it was clear that, with few exceptions, college libraries were unlikely to grow to that point at which their quality would derive primarily from their collections. Not only was the basis upon which to build absent, but the paymasters – college principals, their closest academic advisers, and *their* paymasters – remained to be convinced of the contribution of the library to the institution. In college libraries, therefore, quality should be sought less in the capital resource itself, and more in what is done with it. That is, it is to be sought more in the librarianship than in the libraries.

Second is the view that the college and its members, staff and students, took of the library in the first development phase of many colleges in the 1960s and early 1970s. In Chapter Two, Michael Rowarth notes that many colleges had little view of the library's role. In his words: ' [they] had some difficulty in knowing what to do with them' and ' [their] interest in libraries was perceived as being scant'. Nevertheless, it was felt, if for no readily understood reason, that a college must have a library. This ambivalence, this lack of what the management literature has called 'recipe',[1] derived partly from the strong vocational basis of many college courses and partly from the natural tendency of many college staff and students to experiment and to practise, rather than to read and refer. That, emphatically, is not a criticism. But it does place the onus squarely upon the librarian to prove her/his worth and that of the library service.

Third, there is in the further and higher education sectors an inherent willingness to experiment and to change; to say 'Why not?' and 'Let's try it', when faced with an opportunity or a problem. Colleges have been characterized by enormous change and enormous willingness to accept and promote change. This, along with the lack of a constraining recipe as to the library's 'proper' activities, has helped college librarians create a distinctive identity for their service.

Fourth, librarianship is a profession, and a profession is a vocation. If one has a vocation, one believes that there is an intrinsic value in what one does and that, within reason, more of one's professional contribution is better than less, always providing that the contribution can be tailored to the particular needs of clientele, institution and environment. College librarians believed that their libraries and their professional services had something valuable to offer their college and its members. They felt that, within reason, the benefit would be greater if the library were better and more heavily used, and if it were made an integral part of the academic lives of staff and students.

These influences were not wholly negative. Relatively small collections at least meant that the librarian had time to do other than to service them. The somewhat ambivalent clientele who needed persuading that the library was of benefit to them worked in a climate responsive to change and innovation. The lack of recipe, or view of the library's role, meant that there was little interference from management as to what the librarian must or should do. The intensely practically orientated student body had a pressing need to complete academic assignments successfully; many of these took written form and required the collection and synthesis of information from several sources. All the drawbacks had counter-balancing opportunities.

These features influenced college librarians in their librarianship, in the way the library was promoted to clients, in the role that librarians sought to play in the whole college and in their use of resources. What was their strategy? What were their tactics? What have college librarians done to make their libraries relevant, to make them contributors? What have they done in search of quality? What can give one confidence that college librarianship, with all its acknowledged problems, is a 'quality product'?

The quality strategy

Faced with these elements – small collections; little prospect of their rapid growth; an ambivalent clientele; lack of recipe as to a library's proper activities; a climate responsive to change; a professional desire to provide quality service – college librarians turned to the concepts of fitness for purpose, doing well what they could do, proving their worth and satisfying what demand they could find, while at the same time raising both the level and the sophistication of that demand. The resultant quality strategy might be summarized thus:

- Firstly, to prove that libraries could contribute to the work of members of the college by offering services based upon the skills of the librarian, rather than by providing collections passively and leaving clients to fend for themselves.
- Second, to teach members of the college how to use libraries and the literature effectively, in order to build their belief, confidence and trust in information and libraries.
- Third, to demonstrate that libraries could be an integral part of the education that colleges sought to provide.
- Fourth, to provide material in modes and media most acceptable to clients and to be receptive to and make constructive use of new technologies.

I have not seen the strategy written down thus baldly in the literature, but experience of college librarianship and observation of and contact with many college librarians over an extended period confirm that this was the strategy. It was not covert, but it was unwritten. These principles shaped college libraries and college librarianship and it is within them that the quality of college librarianship is to be discerned. So, college librarians sought their quality spurs through provision of service first, with collections in a supporting role.

The librarian had to convince the college managers, teachers and students, of two things. The first was that the library could contribute at several levels to the sort of practical, pragmatic academic establishment that the college sought to be. The second was that the library, an only partially understood part of the college, wanted and deserved only the same treatment as other parts of the organization – no more, no less, no special favours, but no undue restrictions either; simply a fair share of the rough and the smooth with the engineering department, the art department, the finance office and the rest.

The quality tactics

Let us consider the main headings of the strategy to discover what tactics were employed, what activities were pursued and how these helped the library to add to the quality of the educational experience offered by colleges. Although they are, inevitably, discussed here in a linear manner, in practice each feature influenced and supported the others. This synergy ensured that the whole was/is greater than the sum of the parts.

Access to information

It was necessary to convince clients of the relevance of a library to them, and of its potential to help them. If the library did not hold vast collections on its shelves and could not provide items immediately upon demand, it was willing and able to obtain sought items efficiently and without quibble. If its clients were sceptical about the value of the literature and printed (and later, other forms of recorded) information, the librarian pulled out all the information retrieval stops to prove what the profession could do.

But references retrieved are still only references; the service would only be perceived as valuable by clients once the documents themselves were laid before them. To provide a tangible benefit from the librarian's information retrieval skill, it was necessary to complement the search with supply; there was a financial, as well as a human, cost. College libraries devoted and continue to devote high proportions of their budget and their staff resource to personal service to clients and to buying access to information, online services, CD-ROMs and so on, and to bear the consequent high levels of interlibrary loan costs. This approach has been maintained and study of the breakdowns of the budgets of college libraries[2] reveals high proportions of expenditure on information access, compared with stock purchase. Let us reflect briefly upon the influence and the benefit that Boston Spa has been to this aspect of librarianship in the UK, and acknowledge that it would have been virtually impossible for college libraries to pursue such a policy had it not been established.

The consistent pursuit of this tactic did much to persuade academic staff that the library could help them in teaching, course design, scholarly activities and research. It also helped to convince college management that a good information service could alert them to changes and trends in education, provide intelligence about government plans, regulations and so on, and so support them in policy formulation and in the day-to-day business of running the college. All this helped the college library win acceptance in the staff community, and gave a head start to other quality-orientated tactics and activities.

Today, the approach has its descendant in the much commended 'access before acquisition' approach, in a continuing emphasis on information retrieval and interpreting the library to the client, and in user education. It has made it easier for colleges to embrace CD-ROM hardware and software, for example, despite its high cost relative to their overall budgets. It may also help explain why the libraries of many of the former polytechnics find themselves comfortable with the Atkinson report's concept of the self-renewing library.[3]

Access before acquisition was, to a degree, making a virtue out of necessity, but the tactic was not without risk. Libraries which were comparatively small and financially stretched chose to put a higher than usual proportion of a limited budget into borrowing material and paying for indexes and retrieval services, rather than on purchasing items and building strength on the shelves, thus delaying the point at which they could impress and serve their clientele with a strong collection. The tactic took courage and professional conviction, as well as marketing and communication skills to reach and persuade the client in the first place.

User education

This approach to library service convinced many that there was benefit to them in recorded information – if only one knew how to find it. It persuaded teaching staff to send their students to the library and to require them to use its resources in their work. One-to-one service might be feasible for colleagues on the college staff, but was never a viable proposition for the student body; numbers made that impossible. Hence, user education.

College librarians did not invent user education, but they did much to develop it from a primitive 'Cook's tour' towards the course in lifelong information skills that is common today and they first offered it to a mass market – all the students of a college, rather than a select few. User education in the formal, classroom sense was the useful child of its time, rather than a permanent response. But it served a purpose, and it led to better, more permanent activities.

User education showed students that information could help them in their work and that libraries and bibliographic tools, approached systematically, could yield material which solved problems, shortened preparation time and improved grades. Most college librarians can tell of students whose response changed from 'Why do I have to do this?' to 'Why didn't you show me this before?'. Again, the library proved its potential to contribute.

User education is discussed by Allen Armsby in Chapter 4 and by Ken Watson and Tim Lomas in Chapter 7 of this book. Let us note here that it developed from a process which tried to show people how to use one library – through a phase in which it offered what were, effectively, short courses in the bibliography of the parent discipline of a course – into the concept of lifelong information skills. It has developed from trying to show people how to use the catalogue of one library to wide-ranging information retrieval and information analysis, and study skills, problem solving and personal updating. From an attempt to persuade reluctant students to use a library, it has entered the mainstream of education.

The success that librarians enjoyed with user education did much to enable the current shift from teaching to learning which now sits at the core of the strategic planning of virtually every institution of further and higher education in the UK. It gave college managements confidence that the library offered a support mechanism that would assist students to learn, rather than be taught. Furthermore, it brought librarians into direct interpersonal contact with the client body, helping and requiring the librarian to understand the courses that students enrolled upon, the educational philosophies and techniques that drove these courses, the types of material from which young people found it easiest to learn and the conditions under which they prefer to learn.

Academic planning
Here is the link to the third aspect of the quality strategy. Success

with user education and information provision enabled college librarians to convince their colleagues that they could play a role in course design and educational planning, as well as in the direct support of students. It brought the library centre stage and did much to ensure the librarian's seat at the academic board and in other decision-making fora. This in turn ensured that the library's need to be established and resourced in a manner 'fit for purpose' could be heard and debated, and that the impact upon the library of other college developments and trends could be brought to light.

These three tactics of information access, user education and involvement in academic planning share a common feature; all depend more upon the librarian than upon the library, more upon her/his behaviour and attitudes than upon the collections. This policy of concentrating one's librarianship in the person and the activity of the librarian was successful, but could not of itself satisfy clients and colleges in the long term. The collections had to feature in the quality strategy too. They had to be developed in a manner sympathetic to the other tactics and to the overall strategy.

Multi-media stock

Focus on the collections was the fourth (but not the least) arm of the quality strategy. The collections required special consideration, not just because of their generally small size. The college libraries' ambivalent clientele was as likely to ignore a small collection and find other means of progressing as to regard it as a source of dissatisfaction and hindrance. If clients were offered user education as much to market the library as to explain it, then what they retrieved at the end of the course had better be perceived as interesting, useful and approachable! Therefore, college librarians sought to vary the range and type of material collected and to collect material by subject, level and medium, as well as by pedagogic style.

Amongst print material, books, journals and reports were supported by trade literature, standards, local cuttings and ephemera. College libraries were amongst the first to collect non-print material in quantity: slides, films, illustrations, videos, audio-tape, records and compact discs. In the developmental days of educational technology and programmed learning, college libraries found considerable success with programmed material in text and other formats. This has led naturally to CAL and other software since the microcomputer has made its appearance.

Finally, librarians collected and compiled special collections of material, often of several media, tailored to the needs of particular students and courses. This saw the emergence of the teaching package, its development facilitated by the marriage of subject, pedagogic and bibliographic skills prompted by the close working relationships that had been developed between college librarians and lecturers.

All of this demonstrated the usefulness of the library. To staff, it demonstrated the librarian's ability to tailor her/his skills and practices to the needs of education; to students, it provided a locus in the college where material could be obtained that was both helpful in content and approachable in style.

Monitoring quality

College librarians will recognize all of the above; so, too, will those who have studied, taught and managed in colleges during the last 25 years. Evidence of how the quality strategy has influenced and changed the professional consensus and the formal policy stance of The Library Association, the professional body, is to be found in the several editions of standards and, later, guidelines for college libraries that that body has published over the period.

Earlier editions focused primarily upon resources and stated, fairly baldly, the need for so many books, so much money, so many staff. For example 'number of current periodicals should range from 100 for a small college ... to a minimum of 600 for a college with substantial advanced work'.[4] But even in the first edition, college librarians were showing their hand by including outlines of specimen courses on library use. By the 1980s, the third edition was devoting as much attention to the role of the library and what colleges might expect from it in return for their investment; it states in one of its opening paragraphs, that 'it also includes an indication of the type and quality of service that college managements may expect of their library in return for these resources'.[5] The fourth edition of 1990 goes further, stating bluntly, 'quality in library service depends both upon resources, and upon the use made of them. These *Guidelines* propose a contract between the library and the institution; service should be provided in return for resources received'.[6] The 1990 *Guidelines* also suggest that levels for quantitative provision should be sought, not in the imagination of librarians, but amongst the best actual provision that may be identified in the field. This is echoed by the document which, at time of writing (1993) is the latest such statement to appear; the Scottish Library and Information Council's (SLIC) statement on college libraries[7] follows the policy line of The Library Association's 1990 guidelines, but goes further by being developed by a multi-disciplinary working group including college principals, lecturers and a member of Her Majesty's Inspectorate (HMI), as well as librarians. The very titles of these several publications, when read in chronological order, reveal the shift in stance over time.

If quality may be viewed as improving the nature and value of the educational experience, we are justified in stating that the strategy worked, that college libraries have proved their worth and that they provide a quality service to their parent institutions. Similarly, if quality may be viewed as providing a service that is valued by the client community and provides value to a parent body, then again, the strategy was and is successful.

Nevertheless, it is necessary and proper that quality, in libraries as in other areas of activity, should also be monitored, assessed and if possible demonstrated, by external and impartial means.

The Council for National Academic Awards (CNAA) took a lively interest in the quality of the library in colleges offering courses leading to its awards for several years after it began operation. Many libraries owe their first development steps to its intervention. In the 1960s and early 1970s, it was not unusual for a visiting validation party to include a librarian, irrespective of the subject of the course under scrutiny. Later, this practice stopped, though whether this was because the CNAA decided it could have confidence in all libraries is unclear. At one time, the CNAA proposed standards for libraries in colleges offering courses under its auspices, but these were quickly withdrawn. The CNAA's greatest gift to higher education was its concept of 'partnership in validation', within which colleges and the CNAA collaborated to validate course proposals; this did much for staff development in colleges but, perhaps unfortunately for libraries, it was rare for visiting parties to include library specialists by the time that partnership invalidation was operating. By that time, the CNAA was wont to include them in quinquennial visiting parties, looking at a whole college rather than at any one course. Although their contribution there remained important, the impact was inevitably diluted in a wide-ranging study. Nevertheless, the positive influence of the CNAA on the development of college libraries should not be underestimated.

Given this experience, college librarians had high hopes for the impact upon libraries of the Business and Technology Education Council (BTEC) and the Scottish Vocational Education Council (SCOTVEC) when they adopted the course validation process in the 1980s. However, these two organizations have fought somewhat shy of overt consideration of the quality and nature of libraries and other learning support services in individual colleges. In Scotland, SCOTVEC has received guidance from the Scottish Library Association as to means whereby visitors to a college might reach a view of a library's quality, but at present the manner in which that advice is used remains unclear to librarians in the field. The text of the guidance is an interesting indication of the areas which college librarians regard as exercising the primary influences upon a college library's ability to serve its parent college, and is reproduced with only minor modifications in the recently published Scottish college library standards.[8]

Stepping outside our established field briefly, the recast (i.e., post-1992) higher education sector has seen a plethora of quality monitoring exercises. 'Quality audit' is intended to assess the adequacy of a whole institution's policies and procedures, while 'quality assessment' targets the quality of education offered by individual departments. Sadly, the experience that librarians have had to date (Summer 1993) of groups visiting under these banners is not encouraging; unscheduled visits not aimed at particular staff or functions, random questioning, lack of focus and preparation, and an unwillingness, inability or failure to subject the library to any searching scrutiny have disappointed the profession. One hopes that communication between the Standing Conference of National and University Libraries (SCONUL) and the funding councils will improve matters, and that further education will fare better when the Further Education Funding Council (FEFC) considers assessing libraries, as it surely must.

More searching investigation of library quality has originated in the libraries and colleges themselves. In several of the former polytechnics, the CNAA course validation model has been adapted to provide a means whereby the institution might periodically satisfy itself as to the quality and appropriateness of its library service. Typically, a 'visiting party' including academic staff of the parent college and librarians from sister institutions will meet with a group of library staff from the library under scrutiny to review progress and discuss an agenda agreed between the visitors and the 'home team'. Such events have proved a positive means of directing the attention of both the library and the institution as a whole to issues which might benefit from attention. They provide valuable feedback to the library from representatives of its client group. The functions and operation of such library validation groups in one institution have been recorded by Winkworth.[9]

Since the late 1980s, a Council of Polytechnic Librarians (COPOL) working party has been developing a suite of performance indicators for use in academic libraries. An interim report by Winkworth is available.[10] Throughout this work, COPOL has maintained contact with the funding councils and Her Majesty's Inspectorate (HMI), and it is hoped that, when finished, the results will find wide acceptance. The proposals have the advantage of being based on the long-running COPOL database, which records a range of inputs and outputs for the former polytechnic libraries for the past decade. Here lies its strength; we do not yet know what constitutes quality in absolute quantitative terms; that is, we do not know 'how much is good'. But we can state with some certainty the direction in which a given statistic ought to move if the service is to be perceived as improving; all else being equal, more enquiries answered by library staff are better than fewer, and fewer days' delay between the ordering of a book and its supply are better than more.

Finally in this brief review of college librarians' attempts to monitor quality, it is significant that the Scottish Library and Information Council (SLIC) has chosen to devote almost 33 per cent of its policy statement on college libraries[11] to quality, performance and the importance of assessing these regularly in partnership with senior members of the parent college. It will be interesting to watch the manner in which college managements take up this invitation from the profession.

In the final analysis, it is fitting that libraries themselves should have done more than external bodies to monitor their own performance and quality, and that they should have encouraged others to participate in such exercises with them, for the principle of self-assessment is the key to quality assurance throughout education. College libraries defined their role and their quality stance as being service to and collaboration with the college community and persuaded the college to support their development in this direction. It is fitting that the libraries should now play a lead role in assessing the performance of their quality strategy, still in partnership with representatives of the college community.

The quality strategy reviewed

Can the college librarian's approach to quality be said to have worked? I suggest the answer may be sought by exploring two further questions. Was and is there benefit to clients at a given time? Is there some permanent legacy to librarianship and to education?

The first question is best answered by reference to experience, anecdote and local surveys. Surveys by librarians and the testimony of staff and students indicate consistently that benefit has been perceived by the client and that clients who have been helped once become regular users of the library. Many user education surveys reveal that, once the library had been explained, use of it increased and that higher level of use was maintained. Academic staff have increasingly relied upon the library, not only for themselves but for their students. College management have continued to support their librarians with resources, even if the level remains lower than the librarians would like!

It is easier to give an answer to the question of permanent legacy. It is 'Yes', for three main reasons.

First, the position of the library was strengthened and its role more readily understood by the wider educational community, because the librarian won the confidence of the institution to the extent that s/he is now required to play a wide-ranging role in the academic development and operation of the college: academic board, course development, validation exercises and resource planning, as well as the management of the library itself. In larger colleges and polytechnics, the librarian may spend as much as 66 per cent of her/his time outside the library on institutional planning and management. This is integration, not exploitation, for there is a benefit to the library; it is respected, its needs and contribution are more fully understood by a wider audience and its collections and services are built more closely into the work of students and the scholarly activity of staff.

Secondly, the librarian is involved in the development of both courses and learning materials. The bibliographer works with the educationalist: courses are structured around the availability of resources and resource selection is tailored to meet the needs of these courses. User education has grown into lifelong information skills and has spread far beyond colleges – significantly, into schools. The modern subject librarian works with the teaching staff of a department on collection development. The debate about whether stock should be selected by academics or librarians never took off in colleges because it never became an issue – partnership got there first.

Thirdly, and perhaps most important, the success of the library and the acceptance it won in colleges has supported the development of student-centred learning. This is one of the largest influences upon education in the 1990s, affecting it at all levels from primary school to university. It has implications for lifelong attitudes to learning. It could not happen without support from and understanding of the role of the library and of learning resources.

If the strategy has been successful, why? The skills and practices of one profession, librarianship, were brought into alignment with the aims and practices of another, education; librarians were able to demonstrate that their professional skills and the collections they managed could help fulfil the aims of education and the needs of students. This partnership, even if initially one way, benefited both professions and increased mutual understanding.

Furthermore, the strategy involved all three key aspects of librarianship and gave each a similar degree of importance. Librarians may be viewed as managing a triangular system composed of: clients, who represent demand; stock, which is the library's capital base; and staff, who represent capacity to build and organize stock, and respond to demand. The college librarians' strategy involved all three elements of the triangle and helped librarian and client to understand the relationship between them.

College librarians set out to prove themselves, their libraries and their profession, and to add, through librarianship, to the quality of college education. That they succeeded is evidenced by the manner in which colleges now use their libraries, by the role that libraries now play in the learning of students. The nature of the quality that college libraries provide is perhaps best expressed in The Library Association's guideline *Managing after incorporation: quality.*[12] It seems fitting to let its words close this chapter.

> The library is an integral part of the college; its quality and performance affect everyone and influence the quality profile of the whole institution. The library and the college are accountable together for the library's performance; they should monitor it in an agreed manner and respond to the results observed.
>
> The librarian should arrange for the library to be included in the

college's quality programme, to ensure that the college is resourcing the library adequately to meet the demand placed upon it and that these resources are being used well by librarians.

Quality is easy to recognise, but difficult to define. There are many definitions, but the most readily accepted is that of 'fitness for purpose'. Quality is not about resources alone; it is also concerned with how they are used. Adequate resources are a prerequisite, but do not themselves guarantee quality; policies and attitudes have a great influence. Good practice can be found alongside slim resources; poor services can be demonstrated by resource-rich organisations.

A quality culture, as well as a system, is desirable. Quality is most likely to be achieved by a library which:

a) possesses a rationale and aims to underpin its activities and policies;
b) is service oriented; investigates and responds to clients' needs and helps them to exploit library collections and information resources; generally, adopts principles of good customer care;
c) maintains effective links with the academic and managerial processes of the parent college;
d) understands and responds to changes in education, approaches to learning and the policies of the parent college.
e) passes the scrutiny of peers and reflects the professional consensus as to a library's proper activities.

References

1 Spender, J. C., *Strategy making in business*, Manchester Business School (PhD thesis), 1980.
2 See, for example, the survey carried out in 1992 by SLIC; unpublished, but selected data are available from SLIC.
3 University Grants Committee, *Capital provision for university libraries*, HMSO, 1976. (The Atkinson report)
4 The Library Association, *College libraries; recommended standards for library provision*, Library Association, 1965.
5 The Library Association, *College libraries; guidelines for professional service and resource provision*, Library Association Publishing, 3rd edn, 1982.

6 Library Association, *Guidelines for college and polytechnic libraries*, Library Association Publishing, 4th edn, 1990.

7 Scottish Library and Information Council *and* Scottish Library Association, *Libraries in Scottish further education colleges; standards for performance and resourcing*, SLIC, 1993.

8 *Ibid.*

9 Winkworth, I., 'Performance indicators for polytechnic libraries', *Library Review*, **39** (5), 1990, 23–41.

10 *Ibid.*

11 SLIC, *op. cit.*

12 The Library Association, *Managing after incorporation: quality matters*. (Library Association guideline, 1993)

9

College librarianship and the professional network

Margaret Oldroyd and Robert Oldroyd

Introduction

The role of the Library Association's Colleges of Further and Higher Education (CoFHE) Group is central to the development and success of professional networking in relation to college librarianship. The Library Association itself is the professional body for librarianship, librarians and information staff in the United Kingdom. It has around 25,000 members. Over 2,000 of these are members of the CoFHE Group, a figure which grew steadily during the 1980s. The Library Association's Royal Charter lays upon it responsibility for developing and improving standards of professional practice in librarianship, a principle which also underlies the work of its sectoral groups. The professional network provided by the CoFHE Group is an important means to that end.

The group is characterized by the variety of institutions and the range of professional activity represented in its membership. Members from the 700 or so further education colleges in the United Kingdom work in institutions with student populations which vary from under 1,000 up to 12,000 or more, fte. Courses cover the whole range of vocational and academic qualifications with many offering the first year of degree courses. This mixture of vocational, professional and degree courses also characterizes the higher education colleges. In addition, many members work in the new universities (polytechnics prior to the 1992 legislation) and a number in the older universities, sixth-form colleges, and monotechnics such as the art colleges.

The group has several distinctive features. First, many further education college libraries have only one professional librarian, and few have more than two professional staff. The salary structure in many colleges is such that librarians who are 'junior' (in professional and experiential terms) are often attracted into posts which are relatively 'senior' in terms of responsibility for a major central service, and which require post-holders to negotiate directly with senior management and to compete with heads of other departments for resources. The support needed by this professional group, and the 'one-person unit' syndrome, have been major contributory factors in indicating the direction the group's networking development should take.

Secondly, many further education libraries rely heavily on the skills of their support staff to provide a service over extended opening hours when professional staff cannot be on duty. The Library Association's affiliate member category is intended specifically for these staff, and some 10 per cent of current affiliates are CoFHE Group members.

Thirdly, members both in colleges and new universities are often responsible for converged or integrated services – libraries, audiovisual, computing/information technology, open learning centres, flexistudy units, basic skills workshops, reprographics, to name but a few!

Lastly, but perhaps most important, the Group has members working in every type of post-school academic library in the United Kingdom. These range from the small, single-site, further education colleges, with one librarian and a couple of library assistants, to multi-site higher education institutions with a couple of dozen professional librarians and twice that number of support staff.

CoFHE Group's objectives

In February 1988, the group submitted a report on its work 1982–7 to The Library Association.[1] Its role was defined as 'furthering the development of libraries, librarians and librarianship in college and polytechnic libraries'. The following two groups of objectives, outlined in that report, continue to inform the group's planning, development and activities:

Profession-oriented objectives:
- To develop a consensus view of the principles and objectives of college librarianship, and the pattern of services that should be provided by college libraries.
- To promote that view in cogent arguments for use by The Library Association with employing organizations, government, etc. and/or by individual members in their parent institutions.

- To be represented in fora where matters concerning college librarians may be discussed; failing which, to be consulted on such issues wherever they arise.
- Generally, to contribute to the development, strength and standing of The Library Association both within and outwith the profession.

Member-orientated objectives:
- To identify, monitor, and influence issues concerning the role, objectives, employment, and resources available to college librarians.
- To provide activities, advice, publications, etc., to support members, as librarians and as college staff.
- To involve members in CoFHE Group and Library Association work to increase their understanding of and commitment to both, and to ensure the strength of CoFHE Group, college librarianship, and The Library Association itself.
- To be powerful nationally, but approachable at local level, even to the less confident member.

The emphasis is on college libraries and librarians because that is the sector uniquely represented by the CoFHE Group. The crux of the above is the provision of support through a professional network and quality circles. This in turn provides the basis for achieving the other objectives, in particular the development and promotion of a consensus view to members, government, validating bodies and institutional managers.

How has the Group sought to meet these objectives? Three major areas of activity have formed the bulk of its response: the formation of local and national networks; the provision of continuing professional development opportunities; and the publication of a range of documents and statistics as the basis for a consensus view on good practice in college libraries and librarianship.

Professional networking: local and national

In 1980, the group had only one sub-group or circle, CoFHE Scotland, which for reasons of geography and differences in local political and management structures wished to hold local meetings and had already been in existence for ten years. Members' contact with the group, therefore, was solely through the termly *CoFHE bulletin*, with some 70 members attending the annual study conference. This did not provide a level of contact which enabled the support of isolated members or the involvement of more than a few in professional debate.

In 1980, the London and South East Circle (LASEC) was formed through the efforts of a few members. The circle provided the opportunity to meet locally, and to provide more frequently the professional support and involvement previously found only at conference. During the next two years (1980-2) a revised edition of *College library guidelines*[2] was produced by the group and members of the two circles were involved in the consultation process with the national committee.

Members had found a new means of channelling their experience into a national publication for the benefit of the whole of their sector of the profession. The *Guidelines* adopted a different approach from that of the first edition, emphasizing the dual relationship or 'contract' between a library and its parent college. If the defined level of resources - in terms of staff, funds and space was provided by the college, then a defined level of provision - in terms of stock, services and professional expertise - would be delivered by the library. The discussions between colleagues in the group, with hugely varying levels of experience and institutional background, resulted in the definition of resource and service levels. At the same time, they raised professional awareness, provided stimulating developmental debate, 'cemented' networks and proved that each individual group member could influence the national view of the sector.

By 1983 the group had six regional circles, by 1985, 11, and by 1987, 16. By 1991 all areas of the country (including Northern Ireland) were covered by a total of 18 circles. Many college librarians, especially 'one-person units', find it difficult to leave their service for any length of time to attend conferences. The circles give an opportunity for all to be involved in local meetings - to be part of a professional community. The Library Association is a reality for them, in their area, and their voice is heard at national level.

The national committee has a Circles Liaison Officer (CLO) who helps in setting up circles, and channels information to, from and between circles, often acting as a clearing-house for information (for example, likely speakers on a given topic). New Library Association and/or Group members are put in touch with their local circle by the CLO. Since 1986, the national committee has included seven regional representatives whose role is to provide close liaison and communication between members in a region and the group at national level. Once a year, members of circles' committees and the national committee meet for a day to discuss future plans for meetings, group activities, publications and management. A circles *Handbook*[3] provides guidance on setting up and running a circle and on circle/Group and Group/Library Association relationships. Thus, the 'received wisdom' or the professional consensus is easily passed on, encouraging new or different members to become involved in circle business.

These local CoFHE circles provide fora in which members from further and higher education can discuss topics of common interest and concern, providing mutual help and support. They all organize programmes of workshops, meetings and speakers, some of which result in group publications.[4] If the group is a national quality circle, then these are local quality circles, approachable even to the newest member.

As the circles have increased in number and developed, so the group committee has been able to call upon them for help in the formation of policy statements[5] and the creation of publications[6] both for the group and for The Library Association. They contribute to group comments on proposals from government and help in the collection of statistics and data on college libraries. These have been used, for instance, in the production of a fourth edition of *Guidelines for college and polytechnic libraries*,[7] in the provision by The Library Association of advice on salaries and gradings to individual members, and in the creation of the group's database. The latter consists of a register of expertise and examples of working documents such as annual reports, budgets, aims and objectives, and user education programmes. The involvement of a large number of members, through the circles, has enabled the group to increase and improve the number and range of its responses, publications and activities, thus expanding the quality of service which it offers. The professional quality circles exemplify an upward spiral in which the more people participate, the higher the calibre and range of achievement.

As the cohesiveness and confidence of the Group's network has grown, so it has, in turn, played a greater part in the profession's total network as represented by The Library Association itself. A number of members have stood for election to the Council of The Library Association. In 1991, no fewer than four members of the group's national committee (of 14 members) were councillors and four chairs of standing committees were CoFHE members.

Since 1988, groups have been able to elect a group councillor. CoFHE Group's chairman, Professor Colin Harrison, became its first councillor and was subsequently elected to the chair of The Association's Education Committee (and therefore membership of the Executive Committee). CoFHE Group representatives make a vital contribution to the Academic Libraries Sub-committee (employment), which helps to formulate Library Association policy on salaries, gradings and conditions of service, and which produces the *Salaries guides* for the further education and higher education sectors. A CoFHE representative, Fred Chambers, was Chair of the Sub-committee for a number of years. Members thus contribute to high-level debate on a wide range of issues of professional concern. The *CoFHE bulletin* carries a regular report from the group councillor on council debates. The direct line of communication via regional representatives from circles to group committee to Council enables individuals to feel in touch with The Library Association at all levels.

Here is a direct link with the last of the 'member-orientated objectives' listed earlier; namely, to create a group with national influence which is, none the less, approachable to all, through the local circles. Members can become involved with the group at a level with which they feel comfortable, whatever their stage of professional development. There are clear paths to increase that involvement as and when they wish. At the same time, members who want to maintain contact solely through the local circle are able to do so, confident that views expressed there can be passed on, through national committee and the group councillor, to the highest of levels of The Library Association. Individuals are assured of their ability to have real influence on the Association and more members contribute to policy-making which, in turn, benefits from being rooted in the experience of current practice. In this way, also, a contribution is made to achieving another of the member-orientated objectives – strengthening members' commitment to and understanding of the professional body.

Continuing professional development (CPD) opportunities
A major component of the Group's activities, both locally and nationally, is the provision of a continuing professional development (CPD) programme. Its annual three-day study conference,

which in 1982 was attended by 70 members, now attracts between 150 and 200 participants, including some 60 first-time delegates each year. New circle members are encouraged to attend, while others join a circle after attending conference.

Just as the development of the circles has underpinned the growth in conference size, so its content and organization have evolved to met the changing needs of members. From a somewhat didactic and 'narrowly librarianship' approach in the early days, it has become a much more participative event, emphasizing broader, sectoral themes and with speakers drawn from the wider spheres of educational and institutional management. Current practice study groups – in which delegates discussed topics of concern, shared expertise and gave information and support – have developed into full-scale workshops, led by librarians and others with specific expertise or skills, and requiring full participation. Recent conference themes have included evaluation of library services, personal management skills, the librarian as financial manager, and quality in libraries. Papers have been given by polytechnic and college directors and principals, and chief executives of validation and funding bodies. Horizons are widened and participants given the opportunity to update or develop their professional, political and management skills, supported by their peer group and away from the inevitable stresses of the workplace. Since 1985, the conference papers have been published, thus making them available to a wider audience, including all CoFHE members.

The conference takes place in a different region each year, maximizing the opportunity of access for all, and the appropriate local circle is heavily involved in programme and venue organization. In bringing the national network to the individual in the regions, the cohesiveness of the whole is exemplified and strengthened through the building of personal contacts.

Members have been involved in the writing of, for example, a Further Education Staff College report[8] and a book on college librarianship.[9] They speak at circle meetings and have contributed sessions to the annual International Library Technology Fair programme. The national committee has developed a modular course on management skills for incorporation, which can be run by a variety of leaders, at any venue, using pre-packaged materials. The professional network has provided a means for continuing professional development which, in turn, has enriched the skills available in the network.

Consensus view of good practice

The need to define a consensus view of good practice in college libraries and librarianship underpins many of the activities mentioned in this chapter. The need for the view provides the *raison d'être* for developing the network and for attendance at CPD events. They provide the support which is crucial if individual members are to promote that view locally and nationally.

A number of publications exemplify this approach. The group has stressed the need to influence government, validation and funding bodies by responding to curriculum proposals[10] and White Papers. Guidelines have been developed for both HMI and librarians involved in evaluating institutions and their learning resources services.[11] These have been issued as 'Guidelines' by The Library Association, free to members, and promoted to relevant bodies and individuals. These documents have been written by small groups of members with expertise in particular topics.

The production of the fourth edition of *Guidelines*,[12] published in 1990, exemplifies the evolution of the group's thinking and of its working mechanisms. All the circles were involved in reviewing its first draft. Each workshop at the 1988 annual conference reviewed a chapter of the draft publication. The new edition set the service in the context of the new post-school political and educational ethos, with a new section on evaluation and performance indicators, recognizing government's insistence on demonstrably effective and efficient management, high quality and value for money. The statistics used to suggest resource and service measures were based on a survey of college libraries and represented reality.

A new departure was the simultaneous publication of *Guidelines to Guidelines*,[13] making available the information, comment, working papers and statistics collected during the consultation process which could not be included in the more succinct guidelines document itself. *Guidelines to Guidelines* was intended to make the collective experience of the network available to individual members who used *Guidelines* to promote the development of their services.

Why did the CoFHE Group place such importance on the production and updating of *Guidelines* – a pattern which is now being taken up by other sectors of the profession? In part, this is related to the nature of the membership outlined earlier. Many further education librarians suffer from professional isolation. All, even very early in their professional life, manage a major service. They need to be able to present a strongly articulated rationale for the library and its resource needs to principals and academic colleagues who cannot be assumed to have a ready-made acceptance of the value of the library, certainly not to the extent that it can be expected in higher education. The professional network provides a forum for working out the case and the arguments which support it. A professional virtue is made out of a professional necessity!

Clearly, then, this group has a strong motive for producing *Guidelines*. Members needed them and responded to the imperative to help themselves with their own problems. At the same time, it must be recognized that CoFHE Group members are not the only ones who are professionally isolated and who need to promote the library with non-librarians – many medical and school librarians, for instance, share that isolation. The case for regarding these two factors as the only significant ones is too temptingly neat. Certainly, the development of the group itself through circles and the promotion of continuing professional development and the consensus view were due, in no small measure, to planned activities promoted by many enthusiastic individuals active at local and national level. But while many developments were planned, the fact is that many resulted from the happy coincidence of members with a real and identifiable need being connected to a network of people committed to carrying them through.

Further and higher education network

The 1990 *Guidelines* apply to both college and polytechnic libraries, a change from the 1982 edition, reflecting another development in the network; the increasing cooperation between the group and the COPOL and the University, College and Research Group of the Library Association.

The cooperation between CoFHE Group and groups representing the higher education sector specifically reflects the growing professional consensus on a number of issues relating to academic libraries. The evolution of the further and higher education sectors in the last ten years has been shaped by the government's stress on economy, efficiency and effectiveness in service management. The colleges have followed the polytechnics out of local government control. All are independent; competing for funds from central government; committed to increased student numbers and better quality of provision through strategic planning, improved management, new learning delivery methods, national and local validation, and evaluation frameworks. Higher education is expanding access by franchising its courses through multiple 'outlets', the colleges. The distinction between the further education and higher education sectors becomes more and more blurred.

At the beginning of this chapter, the mixture of CoFHE Group members from further and higher education was highlighted as one of its distinctive features. This has sometimes raised concerns as to whether the professional network could survive such diversity of membership. In fact, its very diversity has been a major strength. Each sector has learned a great deal from (and perhaps more importantly, about) the other. Many false perceptions, both professional and 'personal', have been corrected, particularly with the realization that the similarities far outweigh the differences. Higher education members who have gained expertise in library automation, funding formulae and management for incorporation, for instance, have been able to pass this on to colleagues as these developments came to the further education sector. Similarly, further education members are able to advise their higher education colleagues on open learning, resource-based learning, student-centred learning and customer orientation, where they have long-standing experience. The Library Association's guideline on libraries and franchising[14] was written jointly by members from colleges and polytechnics. This promotes the new edition of *Guidelines*, which is used as the basis for evaluating funding and provision of services in colleges by polytechnic validation parties and provides an approach acceptable to managers both in validating and validated institutions.

The institutions and their libraries may vary in size and name, but the further and higher education librarians' network now represents an integrated and powerful consensus view with which to promote the development of their services. The professional network which is the CoFHE Group has contributed immeasurably to achieving that consensus.

References

1 The Library Association, CoFHE Group, *The work of CoFHE, 1982-1987*, Library Association Publishing, 1988.

2 The Library Association, *College libraries: guidelines for professional service and resource provision*, 3rd edn., Library Association Publishing, 1982.

3 Wallace, Joyce, *CoFHE Handbook for circles*, 2nd edn., Library Association, CoFHE Group, 1991.

4 *Marketing strategies for the academic library*, Elm Publications, 1986.

5 Library Association, *Certificate in prevocational education - guidance note on the role of libraries and librarians*, Library Association Policy Statement, 1986.

6 Mitchell, D. (ed.), *Library buildings*, The Library Association, Colleges of Further and Higher Education Group, 1992. (CoFHE Occasional Publications, 10)

7 The Library Association, *Guidelines for college and polytechnic libraries*, 4th edn, Library Association Publishing, 1990.

8 Further Education Staff College, *Library and learning resources management: current trends*, Further Education Staff College, 1987.

9 McElroy, A.Rennie (ed.), *College librarianship*, Library Association Publishing, 1984.

10 The Library Association, *Certificate in prevocational education*, *op. cit.*

11 The Library Association, *HMI Inspections: a checklist for college librarians*, Library Association Guideline, 1987.

12 The Library Association, *Guidelines*, *op. cit.*

13 The Library Association, Colleges of Further and Higher Education Group, *Guidelines to guidelines: a librarian's companion to the Library Association's Guidelines for college and polytechnic libraries*, The Library Association, 1990.

14 The Library Association, *Library provision for franchished courses*, Library Association Guideline, 1992.

10

Looking to the future

Tom Wilson

To a degree not seen at any other time in this century, legislation has shaped the further and higher education sector in Great Britain. In more relaxed times, committees of inquiry considered and reported, usually at least some moderating influence was brought to bear on the committees while they deliberated, and – after much debate with interested parties – a measured response to their proposals was adopted by local government or the teaching profession itself. *The Education Reform Act* 1990 and the *Further and Higher Education Act* of 1992 (and their equivalents in Scotland) have known little moderating influence from any quarter and have shaped the sector to face certain challenges, not least among these the need for commercial realism, with its emphasis on responsiveness to market forces.

It seems unlikely that fresh legislation will reshape the tertiary education sector within the next ten years. All political parties seem to accept the need for a binary-free system, where student progression has to be freed from unnecessary barriers and individual achievement fostered. This consensus has not yet been conveyed adequately to the general public and so, inevitably, their grasp of what the changes in tertiary education are bringing is incomplete. It may take time for the public to esteem alike both those institutions recently elevated to university status and the traditional universities; it may take time for the public to perceive the effects of incorporation on the further education sector. But it would appear that there is a commitment from both government and opposition parties to securing a prosperous future for tertiary education. Government's determination to ensure that the whole of tertiary education espouses the same standards appears to be its chosen method of ensuring the success of the nation's education and training provision.

What early signs are being detected, then, as a result of such a radical shift in direction - or at least, steer - from a government clear about its intentions? The effects of this present raft of legislation have been predicted by a number of commentators, from trade unionists to serious academics. Among them, many have predicted that the Act must lead to increased competition on the one hand, and to decreased collaboration on the other. The early signs are perhaps less obvious than predicted; change there has been, but it has been incremental rather than fundamental. Colleges and universities have sought to exploit the market-place for their own ends, clearly aware of the risks to sister institutions; but few have forsaken their traditional territory, or pushed out their boundaries towards their neighbour's stronghold. And where there has been worthwhile collaboration, perhaps brokered by the previous controlling authority, mostly those arrangements have continued and strengthened.

But change has come. For the present, it may not have brought with it fierce competition among those striving for territorial gain, but it is producing a tertiary education map markedly different from that pertaining previously. The lead in this has come from higher education and has related to the concomitant increase in student numbers sought by government. More than ever, as higher education reaches for target intakes beyond existing physical capacities, both the new and the traditional universities have forged alliances, often by means of franchises, with further education colleges, most of which had no previous commitment to teaching undergraduate courses.

Such franchise arrangements have put considerable pressure upon the colleges. Even first-degree courses demand a level of resourcing which may stretch the colleges' budgets, along with an investment in staff development which also requires a financial commitment. But perhaps the demands are most obvious in college libraries, where staff have faced both the budget implications of demands to increase stock and the staff development issues of servicing a new client group more immediately than other sectors of colleges. However, in most cases, the demands for improved library services have led to enhanced provision.

So great is the pace of change, as government sets clear targets for participation rates and institutions respond through new partnerships, that one should expect this dynamic interaction of further and higher education to lead to a radical realignment of tertiary education within a shorter rather than a longer period of time.

The further and higher education world of the mid-1990s may well comprise an array of nodal points, to each of which a cluster of institutions will be linked. At those nodal points will be a university which has drawn smaller higher education colleges and a larger number of further education colleges into increasing dependence upon its academic leadership and, equally importantly, its resourcing. Few, if any, of the non-university institutions will be able to resist the pressures to submerge partially their identity for the relative security afforded by university-college status. Initially, the overtures of the university may have limited objectives and may focus on issues such as franchising, articulation and validation, but the long-term implications may be far reaching. Of this, both parties need to be aware. The benefits to both may be considerable, but the likely increase in dependence of the smaller institutions upon their senior partner needs to be recognized by both.

The factors producing the complex weave of collaborative arrangements are many. Increasing student intakes is one, related to obvious, externally imposed targets; others relate to less obvious external pressures. Satisfying external bodies as to quality assurance would exemplify one such pressure. The demands of the kind of validation procedures piloted so successfully by the Council for National Academic Awards (CNAA) are felt keenly in colleges which may have little experience of external validating bodies seeking assurances about quality, either within a course, or across the institution as a whole. Such procedures have been adopted by a number of professional bodies, as well as by other examining and accrediting bodies. At present, it is not unusual for a college to find itself being validated several times in one year by prospective clients, all of whose demands (not always consistent!) have to be met if their qualifications are to be offered. Colleges recognize how onerous such procedures are and are attracted to means of simplifying these time-consuming procedures. The one-door approach offered by the university often allows the triennial validation of that institution to meet the requirements of all the other players. In allowing the university to underwrite the quality standards of its associated colleges, the colleges prepare the way for a closer relationship with the university of their choice. But this relationship should be developed in the understanding of its effects on the autonomy of the colleges themselves. It seems that a likely scenario will see the university as guarantor of quality both within its own walls and beyond them, in its cluster of associated colleges.

For the library service in the smaller colleges, such an academic dependence would bring great benefits. The stage of development of most university library services is such that the university should have few fears about satisfying the requirements of any validating body and inevitably this would draw the associated colleges to aspire to higher standards. The closer collaboration possible within such arrangements would in itself lead to a wider range of services being made available to the student. And for the university, it may also bring benefits: the degree of specialism within a particular associated college may have led to the development of a well-stocked library which would contribute significantly to the enhancement of the library provision within the university-led cluster.

Mergers?

But will the same number of institutions be active in the market-place, or will changing relationships bring takeovers and/or mergers? A number of mergers have already taken place, in both the further and the higher education sectors; few, if any of them, have been the result of one of the parties stumbling in the market-place. In general, they have been attractive to both parties as they sought an enhanced profile in that market-place. Many have felt that there is a critical mass, a size at which an institution is most effective, and that mergers allowed the formation of such a critical mass. It seems likely that the next decade will produce further mergers, most of which will be the mutually agreed outcome of long deliberations or of successful partnerships.

As already noted, many onlookers believe that there is a critical mass below which a university or college cannot maintain viability. Views differ as to what the critical values are, although most agree that they differ, not according to the status of the institution, but in relation to the volumes of activity, perhaps even to the types of activity, in which that institution engages. The argument is advanced that a university with at least a national perspective to maintain on most issues could not down-size and be successful at the level at which an further education college with a local community focus might prosper.

As institutions strive for success or survival in a harsh economic climate, it is inevitable that further mergers will test rigorously the hypothesis that there is an optimum size for an institution occupying a particular place in the complex world of tertiary education. Hopefully too, a body of cases and data will be generated which will allow us to make more objectively informed judgements.

How, during merger negotiations, such political strategies and their economic overtones will affect library provision is not yet clear. One danger would be that the level of service to students and staff, although ostensibly prominent in the preparatory discussion papers, may not prove to be the focus of medium-term attention. In this event, the merged institutions may soldier on with a fragmented library service for several years, while issues less patent to the user are receiving senior management time. Conversely, tackling immediately the unifying of important services which impact on the student would bring immense benefits to the new institution: its student body would perceive the positive side of the merger and its staff would be conscious of at least one clear reminder of further unifying to follow in other areas of service.

Academic drift
At the level of the institution one pressure of which government is aware is what is referred to as 'academic drift'. Over the second half of the twentieth century, several colleges progressed from a local authority funded status to polytechnic and then to university status. The problems that those institutions overcame to cross the binary divide have been well chronicled and the advantages gained are not insignificant. It is possible to detect the early signs of stirring within the newly corporate further education colleges as some seek to fill what they perceive to be a void created recently by the elevation of neighbouring universities. This further stratifying of the further education sector is still possible in a society whose awareness of the fundamental issues distinguishing one college from another is not quite so highly developed as the government's advisers might claim. The danger to present government thinking is compounded by the relatively unsophisticated funding model underpinning further education's activities; the funding model itself appears to lack the ability to resist academic drift, either directly or indirectly, and hardly rewards those institutions who choose to stay firmly and 'purely' within further education. Until there is little disparity in the funding of further and higher education, it is inevitable that colleges with a large proportion of higher education work will look enviously at the status of others and plan accordingly.

The learner

However, the goals towards which tertiary education strives are not all related to status and institutional linkages. There is a discernible focus upon the learner. In that respect, a not-too-distant goal for which further and higher education might strive would seem to be the empowering of the individual learner to design her/his course of study to enable her/him to take that desired next step in progression towards her/his goal. The implications for the counselling services of the institutions are grave and those of managing resources to meet the demands of a discerning client group no less so; if the clients are to exercise a growing degree of autonomy in course design, both strategic and operational issues have to be faced. Strategically, the institution will have to espouse credit accumulation and transfer wholeheartedly and provide for learners routing themselves through individually tailored programmes. For libraries and other front-line service deliverers – face-to-face with the enlightened, empowered and demanding student – the liberating of the learner will provide the acid test of operational soundness. One major pressure the library service faces is living with and honouring its mission of serving the individual; easier far to serve the corporate body!

All political parties seem to accept the need for a binary-free system where student progression has to be freed from unnecessary barriers and individual achievement fostered. It would appear that they will not balk at achievements which do not lead to one of the existing group awards society has previously recognized or respected. This openness to the creation of new and innovative programmes is already evident in the proliferation of new course titles offered by the new universities and it will blossom further, leaving the careers counsellor with a perplexing range of choices to offer to the prospective student. The assembly of information to assist the enquirer, whether s/he seeks a set programme or wishes to plan her/his own programme, will inevitably involve the library service.

There is in the early 1990s a growing awareness that the gaining of a degree or diploma is not to be seen as the end of the learning process, but as a significant step along the pathway of lifelong learning. The oversupply of labour over the demands of the employment market has heightened that awareness; the tariff required by the employer has increased at least proportionately with unemployment. For those in work, personal and continuing professional development is accepted as essential to ensure future and lucrative employment. For those out of work, retraining is often the remedy offered. The prognostication for employment rates leads the observer to expect among graduates and diplomates a responsiveness to updating that exceeds present expectations. Decidedly, one factor influencing institutional development will be the continuing development of those in and seeking employment. No longer will institutions be only pre-service educators.

Libraries in many institutions were not designed or developed to support continuing professional development and may initially seem inadequate to the task. They may lack interactive workshop facilities and state of the art audiovisual technology; perhaps the physical design of accommodation will be lacking. But the professional service provider will readily overcome these difficulties in time.

Services to industry

Available in any college or university is a range of equipment, facilities and ability which is not always tapped by industry and the wider society. The reasons for the lack of uptake are rooted more in perceptions of the public sector's role than in either the cost of those services to the user, or the responsiveness of the provider. Little by little, these perceptions are changing, so much so that it can be confidently predicted that over the next decade the services of colleges and universities will feature prominently in the marketplace. Not least among these services will be the library service, an arm of which is likely to function commercially, marketing services to a range of clients who do not have access to a professionally run and adequately resourced library. The range of services available already is extensive and growing; professionally marketed, this will prove attractive in the eyes of many companies.

Involvement with a growing number of commercial clients will affect the nature of the library service. Library staff are already client-orientated in their approach, but dealing with companies buying services will no doubt sharpen perceptions as to what the value of information is and accordingly improve, at least marginally, the approach of the parent institution itself to the provision of library services for internal use. The influence of commercial realism as exercised by clients will be felt much beyond the library itself.

Technology

At the beginning of this decade, the vice-chancellor of Cranfield

Institute of Technology pointed up the dilemma facing one specific area of human endeavour – electronics. In 1990, as he spoke, knowledge was doubling every 2.5 years, so that ten years after graduating the electronic engineer was dealing with a knowledge base of which 80 per cent had not been discovered when he completed his degree. The pace of knowledge growth is unlikely to slow in the next decade and so, inevitably, libraries will face even greater demands in fulfilling their role as access points to knowledge. Certainly until now, the only answer to the pace of knowledge growth has been provided by the parallel growth of technology applications in the library service.

The great thrust forward of the 1980s found its impetus in the converging of three previously distinct disciplines – electronics, computing and telecommunications. Their convergence brought to us cheap storage devices like CD-ROM and disc to allow all but the humblest library to provide in portable and accessible form that which hitherto had required many years to collect, many cubic metres of valuable space to store and many tedious hours to search. There arrived too, at only the cost of a telephone call, linkage to sophisticated networks and databases through which enquiry could yield the information that the specialist user required. Thus, even modest budgets were stretched to bring meaning to global strategies, networking colleagues in far-off continents so that their resources might be shared.

Clearly, the libraries of the twenty-first century will continue to be mainstream users of the technologies that feature so largely at the moment. But librarians will remain committed to exploiting every further opportunity the emerging technologies bring within grasp. Already, advances in fibre technology are allowing voice and data to be transferred along the same pathway, with obvious benefits and savings to the user. That comparatively simple step will bring within reach a learning environment within which the full resources of our finest libraries can be accessed interactively by the learner to a degree not yet seen. True multi-media resourcing will then be the accepted norm in every college and university. Student expectations will continue to rise; their expectations will embrace the higher standards of presentation that multi-media offer, both within the lecture-room and from libraries and learning workshops. Students will also expect to be able to assemble multi-media presentations where in the past a written essay would have been thought adequate.

Looking ahead

Not too distant is the virtual campus, where each student can access electronic resources and interact with others beyond the bounds of the physical campus. The constraints of timetabling produce in well-motivated learners a sense of frustration that they cannot pursue a particular theme because responsibilities at work or at home require their involvement at the very time they should be in a classroom some miles away. Only technology offers the possibility of minimizing the constraints of time and space to allow the learner to learn at the pace and at the place of her/his choice. And if the part-time market is to expand as government desires and insists it will, then the answer to this demand-led client group will lie, not in more face-to-face classes taught at fixed times, but in putting the learner centre stage and building for her/him bridges to the resource-based learning s/he needs.

At present, despite the growth in the number of students engaged in flexible learning programmes, the proportion of learning being pursued in this mode in colleges or universities is still comparatively small, in some instances less than 1 per cent. Many institutions are already planning for a dramatic increase in this statistic in the next few years.

However, the needs of the remote user of education services may not mean s/he will be content to pursue studies without being physically present on campus at any time. Given the need for interaction with others, as the Open University (OU) and other providers for remote-access students have found, there is a place for bringing together such students from time to time for workshops and seminars. It may well be that the design of libraries will need to take account of the particular needs of such a visiting population. Small, well-appointed seminar rooms adjoining the library or its reading rooms may be an answer in part to the needs of a new client group.

An international dimension

The higher reaches of academe have accepted for many years the exchange of ideas among colleagues from countries outwith the United Kingdom. The growing influence of the single market and the availability of European Community funds to assist in student and staff exchanges within the EC have seen the development of collaboration among European colleges to a degree not previously possible. But interest in colleges in countries outwith the European

Community has grown too. In particular, the community college, as developed in the USA, has attracted attention from senior college managers in Britain, who recognize the success of a system not unlike that to which they believe British tertiary colleges now belong. This internationalizing of college education is a relatively new phenomenon and one whose effects should be gauged by planners.

How will it influence students? Many European and American colleges have embedded the principle of students studying abroad for part of their course. This principle is essentially an extension of the Credit Accumulation and Transfer Scheme (CATS) developments already discussed and is proving attractive to students. Providing there is no deepening of the economic gloom which has limited the scope for such innovative steps, it seems likely that growing numbers of students in a number of countries will become involved in exchange schemes.

There could be at least two repercussions for college libraries. First, it is likely that the more imaginative and highly developed institutions would be in the forefront in pioneering such linkages; for that reason, their students will bring with them to linked colleges experience in another, and probably highly developed, library. Clearly, the receiving institution would feel under pressure to absorb the good practice of the twinned college and develop its own library accordingly. Secondly, especially where English is a second language to the overseas students, the receiving college is likely to seek to support its visiting students with such enhancements as learning materials in their language, as well as EFL provision. Such multi-lingual software may later offer other commercial benefits to the college by attracting custom for the new software and forging new links to be exploited.

Student-centred still

Over the last 30 years, student expectations have risen: students know the level of accommodation they require; they expect the current technologies to be adapted to their needs; they recognize acceptable standards of customer care. It is unlikely that the learners of 30 years hence will be any less demanding; most colleges are planning for the enhanced level of service they believe will be enshrined in the developing student charters of future years.

The reshaping of library services in any college or university until now has been led by staff rather than students; students may have agitated for, and subsequently influenced, change; but the main agents of change have not been from within the student body. The early signs of a power-shift are evident; by the end of the decade this shift will have empowered learners to determine the shape and level of service that should be provided by the college or university. Both strategic and operational planners require to note the degree of change already evident and to ensure that appropriate mechanisms are in place to allow students to move for changes in the service they require.

For all engaged in the learning or teaching process, the last 15 years have brought great advances in pedagogy and curriculum delivery, which, coupled with institutional and legislative change, have stimulated debate and led to the reappraisal of almost every aspect of post-compulsory education and training. Initially, it may have been reluctantly that the exercise of reappraisal began, but thereafter the value of scrutinizing all aspects of provision has been appreciated by both senior managers and their staff. The entrants to the new further and higher education of the mid- to late 1990s and beyond will encounter a no less vigorous debate and no less stringent re-evaluation of the provision in which they are engaged. There may be changes in emphasis over the remainder of the decade, but the vibrancy which has characterized tertiary education over the previous two decades will not diminish. This, at least, is our bequest to new cadres of staff and students; in the library services of tertiary education that vibrancy will remain evident.

In conclusion

There are times when every busy professional has to betake her/himself to some vantage point from which to survey the developing scenes in which s/he is involved. The changes being noted may not be merely incremental, but their full significance and their cumulative effects may not be grasped until seen in perspective. One of the obvious needs is for opportunity to be given to college librarians to distance themselves for a time from the daily routine of assessing this change and that demand, in order that they may be able to consider how so many factors have converged upon their area of responsibility and be the better able to chart the way ahead for college libraries.

One would expect that primary among the conclusions such considerations might yield would be the recognition that the librarian of tomorrow is not recognizably the same as yesterday's curator of books and guardian of silence. At once the college librarian is a respected collaborator with academic colleagues, one whose professional skills provide an entry into every academic forum in the college, the supporter of every learner, young and old, and a practitioner involved with sophisticated computer services and electronic materials. But the demands do not end there. The librarian is expected to exercise marketing *nous* and flair; s/he must ensure that the client finds her/his needs met by a client-centred service, which promotes its services; s/he must ensure that the client can depend on its (the library's) staff to meet the highest level of expectation. The professional, educational, managerial and entrepreneurial abilities implied by this should not be underestimated by any. The continuing development of staff requires to be considered by senior institutional staff and their professional advisers.

But the enhancing of any service rarely lies entirely with its staff; often another hand controls the flow of funding. Being no different in that respect from the heads of many other funded services, librarians will add to their many roles that of lobbyist to ensure that the case for planned investment in stock, in electronics and in suitable premises is heard by decision-makers, most of whom are not averse to library expansion but are confronted with competing demands for scarce resources.

Few would wish the college of tomorrow to be a pale shadow of even the best of yesterday, but not all realize that one of the great levers for change lies in the library. Without it providing appropriate services, the didactic approaches of a past era will continue; the dependence of the learner upon the lecturer will remain through an uninspiring tracking process, leading inevitably to embarrassing drop-out rates and underachievement. Librarians should ensure that all recognize the importance of their service to the responsive college of the future.